BIBLICAL
INSPIRATION

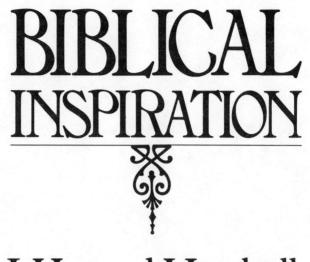

I. Howard Marshall

WILLIAM B. EERDMANS PUBLISHING COMPANY
GRAND RAPIDS, MICHIGAN

First American edition published 1983 through special
arrangement with Hodder and Stoughton by
Wm. B. Eerdmans Publishing Company, 255 Jefferson Ave. S.E.,
Grand Rapids, Michigan 49503

Reprinted, February 1985

Library of Congress Cataloging in Publication Data

Marshall, I. Howard.
Biblical inspiration.

1. Bible — Inspiration.   2. Bible — Criticism,
interpretation, etc.   I. Title.
BS480.M334   1983   220.1'3   83-1427
ISBN 0-8028-1959-1

CONTENTS

PREFACE

A wise man whose authority and truthfulness will be quite unaffected by anything written in the following pages has declared that 'the way of transgressors is hard' (Pr. 13:15). The path of anybody who dares to express his views on the nature of the Bible is particularly hard because his path does not run merely along the edge of a cliff with the sea down below on one side; he is traversing Striding Edge with the possibility of going astray both to the right and to the left (Pr. 4:27). Should I so much as deviate to the left and suggest that not all that Scripture says is true in the strictest sense of that term, I shall come under strong criticism and possibly even excommunication from the right, not simply for saying so, but for saying so as a confessed evangelical; and should I throw in my lot unreservedly with my colleagues on the right, I shall undoubtedly suffer at the hands of my colleagues on the left, who will doubt not only any claim that I dare make to be a biblical scholar but also my sanity. I take my life in my hands, therefore, and I trust that what I write will be seen as an attempt to state the problems of biblical truth and authority in a constructive and sympathetic manner.

What follows is a considerably enlarged and rewritten form of two lectures which I was privileged to give in Wycliffe Hall, Oxford, in November 1981, and which constituted the first of an annual series of lectures in memory of W. H. Griffith Thomas, who was Principal of the Hall from 1905 to 1910. I take this opportunity of expressing my thanks for this invitation and for the gracious hospitality which I received.

I should also like to express my thanks to the countless people who have helped me to think over the problems discussed in this book over many years, and in particular to my wife Joyce and to David F. Wright, Senior Lecturer in

Ecclesiastical History in the University of Edinburgh, for their comments on my manuscript.

I. Howard Marshall
March, 1982

INTRODUCTION: THE PROBLEM

If you go to a service in almost any Christian church, it is probable that at some point the person who is conducting it will read aloud to the congregation one or more passages from the Bible; he may introduce them with some such words as 'Hear the Word of God, as it is written in the Scriptures of the Old Testament, in the Book of Genesis, chapter three and verse one.' This announcement sums up a problem that sooner or later we all have to face as Christians. What does it mean to say that the Bible is the Word of God? There are many different answers to the question.

At the one extreme, there are the people who do not find that there is any problem, at least as far as their own beliefs are concerned. They have been brought up to believe that the Bible is a book written ultimately by God through the pens of human writers, so that everything which it contains is the Word of God, and the existence and character of the human authors is almost irrelevant. The Bible as it stands is a divine revelation, and therefore it is to be implicitly believed. Sometimes fun is poked at people who confess that they believe whatever the Bible says. 'Do you really believe that the whale swallowed Jonah?' was the question put to one friend of mine, and she answered, 'I'd believe what the Bible says, even if it said that Jonah swallowed the whale!' One hopes that the answer was given with tongue in cheek. Joking apart, however, many people accept implicitly that what the Bible says is true and beyond question, and that therefore they must follow its teaching.

On the other hand, there are people who regard the Bible more as the record of mankind's religious quest and experience, a book of essentially human questions and human answers. Few people, even among non-Christians, would want to deny that the questions are concerned with genuine human needs and searches, or that the answers given contain elements of truth; even atheists and adherents to other religions are ready to admit that there is some value in the Bible, although for them it is in this respect no different from any other human book. Christians who stand towards this end of the spectrum generally assert that in some way God reveals himself at different points in this collection of human books. From time to time, they say, the human writers offer what has the ring of truth, although at other times the records are painfully self-contradictory and erroneous.

In between these extremes there are a host of other positions, some simple, some complex, which attempt to do justice to this two-sided character of the Bible as being man's words and yet somehow God's Word. Often the answer takes the form that the Bible is the human record of a divine revelation which took place in the history and experience of the people of Israel and, above all, in the coming of Jesus. Imperfect and at times erroneous though the record may be, it can nevertheless guide us to our own experience of God and through it we can hear the Word of God to us.

One may well be bewildered by the sheer variety and amount of discussion of the Bible, especially as it shows no signs of coming to a standstill. Recent years have seen five main developments. First, a number of writers, mainly but not exclusively from North America, have reiterated in the strongest possible terms the traditional conservative position that the Bible is God's infallible Word throughout. Fearful, however, lest the traditional description of the Bible as merely 'infallible' should allow Christians to adopt a view of it which does not do full justice to its character as a book inspired by the Spirit of God, they have claimed that the mark of genuine, orthodox Christianity is acceptance of the Bible as 'inerrant': it is 'without error or fault in all its teaching, no less in what it states about God's acts in creation, about the events of world history, and about its own literary origins under God, than in its witness to God's saving grace in individual lives'. These words are taken from 'The Chicago Statement on Biblical Inerrancy' which is a recent, authoritative exposition of this point of view. Within a short time there has grown up a considerable literature criticising and defending this position. It is a debate which has taken place within the circle of evangelical Christianity, and it has had some regrettable consequences in promoting a certain distrust between Christians who hold varying views on this matter. (For the Chicago Statement see N. Geisler (ed.), *Inerrancy*, Grand Rapids, 1979, pp. 493–502; J. I. Packer, *God has Spoken*, London, 1979, pp. 139–55.)

Secondly, there has been a resurgence of criticism of the whole evangelical position reminiscent of the 'fundamentalism' debate of the 1950s. The protagonist in the attack is James Barr, himself a former adherent to a much more traditional position, whose book *Fundamentalism* (London, 1977) is a shrewd, wide-ranging and (it must be confessed) sometimes intemperate attack on the whole position which he identifies as 'fundamentalism' and on its understanding of the Bible in particular.

Thirdly, attention has been drawn to the wide cultural gap between the world of the biblical writers and the world of today. In his book *The Use and Abuse of the Bible* (London, 1976), D. E. Nineham has stressed the extent of this gap and argued that the Bible is almost unusable today since its way of thinking is so different from ours. We cannot, in his opinion, use the Bible directly, simply as a source of divine revelation and teaching. While it is clear that Nineham does not deny that God can speak today through the Bible, it is unfortunate that the main thrust of his work is negative.

Fourthly, various fresh attempts are being made from a middle-of-the-road position to approach constructively the problems raised by the Bible. Scholars have been re-examining traditional views of the nature of the Bible in order to find new ways of expressing them in a manner that will take account of the findings of modern study. Such work can only be welcomed. It is the constant task of Christian scholars to examine the doctrines of the Church and to re-express them for today. The subject of biblical inspiration has been tackled in several books, among which W. J. Abraham's *The Divine*

11

Inspiration of Holy Scripture (Oxford, 1981) may be particularly singled out as an attempt to provide a constructive statement along traditional lines.

But a fifth development is perhaps more important. It has become increasingly obvious that the question of how we are to interpret the Bible is of central significance in discussing its character as the Word of God. From all sides there has come a spate of works on how to understand and interpret the Bible. Here one may mention the brief, but stimulating, essay by A. C. Thiselton, 'Understanding God's Word Today', in one of the collections of essays produced in connection with the National Evangelical Anglican Congress in 1977 *Obeying Christ in a Changing World* (edited by J. Stott).

Even this brief survey of recent discussion – painfully inadequate though it is – may be sufficient to indicate how widespread and fundamental are the problems which beset the Christian today who starts to think about the nature of the Bible, and how varied are the answers which are given. The Bible does pose some very real problems to its readers, and we do ourselves no service either by pretending that there are none or by capitulating in face of the difficulties. My aim in this book is to try to produce a positive statement of the nature of the Bible in the light of the difficulties that face readers today.

1. First, there is the large question of how God reveals himself to mankind. Some people may well want to begin further back with the question of whether there is a God at all. Even within the Christian Church one can find people who want to ascribe the highest honour to Jesus as the embodiment of supreme love and self-sacrifice and yet to deny that there is a God or that Jesus is his Son. However, to embark on a discussion at this level would be to divert us seriously from the task envisaged for this book, namely to consider how the God of orthodox Christian theology reveals himself to us. In other words, I propose to conduct the debate on the assumption that my readers share a belief in the reality of God, the Father of the Lord Jesus Christ. I am presupposing that God has

12

revealed himself supremely in Jesus Christ, the historical person who lived and died, who rose from the dead, and who is a spiritual reality to his followers in every age. It is perfectly proper to discuss the validity of this belief, but this book is not the place to do so.

If, however, God has revealed himself through the person and life of Jesus, the question arises whether he reveals himself in other ways. In particular, can he reveal himself through a collection of books written by human hands? There are some Christians who would deny this possibility. They would accept that God revealed himself through historical events in which people could see his hand at work, and they would stress that, if God is personal – i.e. if the most appropriate language for us to describe him in is that which we apply to persons – then revelation must be essentially personal in character and it took place in Jesus. Revelation, to put it otherwise, takes place in personal encounter and cannot be reduced to written statements; these can at best be witnesses to revelation but are not themselves revelation. The Bible, then, is not to be understood as a communication from God to men.

Although this position was defended by some notable theologians in the past, one hopes that it has now been finally laid to rest. Like many other theories it is right in what it affirms and wrong in what it denies. It is certainly right to affirm that revelation took place supremely in the person and life of Jesus Christ and also in the historical experience of the people of Israel and of the early Church, and the Scriptures do function as a record of these historical acts of revelation. But it is wrong to deny that the Bible itself can be a form of revelation, and it is at this point that the view we are considering runs into insuperable obstacles.

The first of these is that Christian experience demonstrates that for many people the Bible has in fact been a vehicle of encounter with God. Revelation is certainly personal encounter with God. The fact is that Christians do experience such moments of revelation as they read the Bible. It becomes the means through which God is able to speak directly and make himself known to them.

The second obstacle is that, if the Bible is merely the record of other people's encounters with God, then it is not easy to see how what happened to them can happen again in our lives. Somehow the original encounter has to come alive again for us, or there has to be a fresh encounter with God. But it is difficult to see how a mere record can produce either of these effects. If, however, the Bible itself is a form of revelation, then it can function to bring us into the same situation as the actors in the story or to create a fresh situation of revelation for us.

The third obstacle to this view is that it misunderstands the nature of revelation. If an event reveals God it is because a certain interpretation or explanation of that event is accepted by the person who experiences it or reads about it. The interpretation no doubt arises out of the event, for otherwise it would not be a true interpretation, but the interpretation is needed to explain the significance of the event. Without interpretation the event is not an act of revelation, and least of all is it an act of revelation to somebody who did not experience it and does not know how it was originally experienced. Interpretation is an integral part of the act of revelation, inherent in the act for the original recipient and essential as its accompaniment for each new recipient. In practice the account of the event and the interpretation of it are usually one and the same thing, and it is hard to dissociate them. So the point is that revelation for us takes place through interpreted events, and the interpretation must take place in words.

The fourth obstacle to the view which we are criticising is that it misunderstands the significance of words and speech by regarding them as something less than personal. In fact speech is one of the most characteristic activities of persons by means of which personal relationships are made possible. Whether or not intelligent apes can be taught to practise a rudimentary kind of speech, as recent experiments have suggested, is not the point. The vital issue is that without fully developed powers of speech real personal relationships are impossible. To deprive God of the opportunity to speak to his creatures, using words that they can understand, would be to reduce him to a subpersonal level, something less than the God and Father of our Lord Jesus Christ. Logically, it would also involve the conclusion that we cannot pray to him and address him in speech as well.

During a period of hostilities a man who was being kept as a prisoner of war managed to get a copy of a message sent to his wife assuring her that he was alive and expressing his love to her. Consider the situation of the wife. The message in words came across the miles to her and acted as a revelation of the continuing reality of her husband's love and concern for her. To her it made up for his absence and was the next best thing to what she wanted most, to be reunited with him. It could have been a forgery, but she was prepared to believe it. It was brief and inadequate, and copied by another hand than her husband's, but it sufficed. She would not have wanted to say that it was impersonal and that nothing but a personal meeting with her husband would do. Nor could the message and the concern which it embodied have been conveyed in any other way than by words, or by some other form of personal expression. Words are essential and words suffice. Even if the husband was released and returned home to his wife, one can hardly imagine that their meeting would have taken place in total silence and apart from words. In short, to say that God cannot make use of words and statements to reveal himself is to go against all that we know of persons and how they relate to one another.

I conclude, therefore, that the possibility that God uses words to reveal himself is thoroughly reasonable, and if he does not do so, it is very dubious whether he can reveal himself at all adequately to us. In what follows, I propose to assume this point.

2. Secondly, we have the question whether the Bible is the means through which God reveals himself to us. This question contains a number of elements. Obviously it is necessary to ask how the Bible, which is ostensibly a collection of books by human authors, can be at the same time the vehicle of the

Word of God. Are we to identify the words of the Bible with the Word of God? And if so, is some of the Bible God's Word or all of the Bible? By what means can a book be at one and the same time a human composition and yet the Word of God? Or is this an altogether wrong way of envisaging the matter? We face the question of the nature of the Bible.

3. Even if we can produce a theory of how the Bible may be the Word of God or function as the Word of God, there is the question of how we can know whether the theory is true. In what ways, if any, could we prove or demonstrate that the Bible is a vehicle of God's revelation of himself to mankind? Indeed, is it a matter of proof at all?

4. There is no denying that there are many difficulties lying in the way of accepting the Bible as the Word of God. It is a collection of books written over a period of many centuries, and there are, to say the least, apparent contradictions between what is said in different parts. It does not require much ingenuity to read through the parallel accounts of the same historical period in the books of Kings and Chronicles and to discover all sorts of minor discrepancies between them. The reader of, say, Leviticus, Proverbs and Philippians might conclude that he was dealing with documents from three rather different religions. Even in the New Testament the pictures of Jesus in Mark and John show some surprising differences.

Again, it is not difficult to find statements whose historical reliability is open to question. Historians are still puzzled as to how to fit the account of the exodus of the Israelites from Egypt and their conquest of Canaan into the framework of secular history. The statements that Jesus was born before the death of Herod and after the census of Quirinius are apparently contradictory. Further, much of the Bible does not look like divine revelation. It certainly does contain what purport to be statements by spokesmen for God, but much of it is of a different character, including many statements addressed *to* God. And what do we make of the long lists of

16

ancient peoples and their relationships to one another in the early chapters of Chronicles, or of the frankly erotic poetry that we find in the Song of Solomon (and that we probably refrain from reading publicly in church)? Not to mention the various stories in the Bible that may seem quite incredible today. There are miraculous events of various kinds, some of them impressive and significant, like the raising of Jesus from the dead, others of them apparently banal and trivial, like the ability of a prophet to make an iron axe-head reappear on the surface of a stream into which it had accidentally fallen.

Some people are prepared to believe whatever the Bible says simply because the Bible says it, or rather because in their view whatever the Bible says, God says, and that's the end of the matter. Such an attitude to the problems in the Bible arises out of a prior belief that the Bible is God's Word; whether it is satisfactory is another matter, and one may say that people who do accept the Bible in this way still have a responsibility to give some explanation of how they square these things with their belief. But if we are approaching the Bible from a position of uncertainty about its character, looking for evidence to help us to come to a responsible conclusion, then we cannot sweep these problems aside in making our assessment of the Bible, but must face up to them honestly.

5. Finally, a whole group of problems arises when we consider how to understand the Bible. If the Bible is the Word of God, it may strike us as strange that there seems to be so little agreement on how to interpret its teaching. Even if the major Christian denominations may agree on some of the main lines of biblical teaching, yet their views on other aspects of it are so varied and so tenaciously defended that they prefer to retain their independence and cannot come to a common mind. Within any one denomination or even any single group of Christians there can be sharp disagreements over what the Bible actually teaches. When one fills out the picture with the idiosyncratic views of the many sects and individuals which differ from 'mainline Christianity', the problem emerges all

17

the more clearly. Can a book which is open to so much variety in understanding and often to sheer misunderstanding really be God's intended means of revelation to us? Christians often talk about the authority of the Bible, but how can so confusing a book serve as an authoritative exposition of God's will for us?

This is by no means a complete listing of all the problems that could be raised. The present writer must confess to being at the more conservative, orthodox end of the theological spectrum, and therefore critics could argue that he is constitutionally incapable of perceiving the problems in all their strength and complexity. Nevertheless, the problems are there, and we must endeavour to come to grips with them. Our discussion in the following chapters will attempt to cover them more or less in the order in which we have raised them.

1

WHAT DOES THE BIBLE SAY ABOUT ITSELF?

Strictly speaking, the question 'What does the Bible say about itself?' is not very well expressed. The phrase 'the Bible says', which became a well-known expression as a result of its frequent use at public meetings by Dr Billy Graham, is really a piece of shorthand. For the Bible is a collection of books by various authors, each of whom may deal with particular themes that are not discussed by the others. And of course books do not actually 'say' anything; it is their individual writers that do so. When people use the phrase 'the Bible says', therefore, they are really referring to statements by the individual authors of different books in the Bible that may reasonably be regarded as expressing the general sense of the several writers. If, then, we ask 'What does the Bible say about itself?' we must bear in mind that none of the biblical authors refers specifically to all of the books of the Bible, although we may find statements in parts of the New Testament that refer generally to the books of the Old Testament (e.g. Luke 24:27, 44). What we are concerned with is the general sense of the statements made by individual writers regarding what they regarded themselves and their colleagues as doing.

Since an exhaustive survey of the evidence would be impossible, let us take one or two quite typical examples. If we turn to the book of Jeremiah, we find that it begins like this:

The words of Jeremiah, the son of Hilkiah, . . . to whom the word of the Lord came in the days of Josiah . . . Now the word of the Lord came to me saying, 'Before I formed you in the womb I knew you, and before you were born I consecrated you; I appointed you a prophet to the nations.'

> Then I said, 'Ah, Lord God! Behold, I do not know how to speak, for I am only a youth.' But the Lord said to me, 'Do not say, "I am only a youth"; for to all to whom I send you you shall go, and whatever I command you you shall speak. Be not afraid of them, for I am with you to deliver you, says the Lord.' Then the Lord put forth his hand and touched my mouth; and the Lord said to me, 'Behold, I have put my words in your mouth . . .'
>
> (Jer. 1:1–9)

After this the book continues with accounts of how the words of God came to Jeremiah and quotations of what God said, accounts of things that God told Jeremiah to do and how he did them, together with accounts of what Jeremiah said to God and stories about Jeremiah sometimes told in the first person and sometimes in the third person.

The book thus contains a mixture of various kinds of material. There is a narrative told in the first person by Jeremiah himself as he describes his own experiences, and there are also stories told about Jeremiah by an unknown narrator. Much of the book consists of accounts of what Jeremiah heard as 'the Word of the Lord' and which he then passed on to those who would listen to him. So far as Jeremiah's understanding of the matter is concerned, we could distinguish between the words of God which came to him in some kind of personal experience, and which he then passed on to his hearers, and the words spoken or written by himself and other people which could be regarded as ordinary human utterances. The book of Jeremiah is a record of the career of a prophet who proclaimd the words of God, but its contents are not confined to such words of God.

If we look elsewhere in the Bible, we should find the same general picture. In Paul's second letter to the church at Corinth, for example, we find that for the most part he writes in the first person expressing what he has to say to his friends there. At one point, however, he describes how he was moved by an affliction to pray to God that it might be removed from him, and then he records in words what God said to him as the reply to his prayer (2 Cor. 12:9). Again, as in Jeremiah, we can distinguish between the words directly spoken by God and the human words of Paul which constitute the bulk of the letter. To be sure, Paul can on occasion give judgments which he regards as having the backing of the Spirit of God (1 Cor. 7:40). He can even say that Jesus Christ speaks through him – and not merely when he is writing letters (2 Cor. 13:3). Elsewhere he claims that when he preached the gospel at Thessalonica his converts accepted what he said 'not as the word of men but as what it really is, the Word of God' (1 Thess. 2:13).

One would be rash to generalise and say that every time that Paul said anything or wrote anything he would claim that Jesus Christ was speaking through him. Nevertheless, he was very conscious of possessing a special commission and authority that enabled him to declare what God was saying to his people. He appears to be in the same position as Jeremiah, who spoke both on his own account and also on the Lord's account.

These two examples could be multiplied, but the resulting picture would not be essentially different. The books of the Bible contain what are clearly regarded as the words of human actors telling about human actors and on occasion reporting what people said to God. They also contain what are identified as the words of God, sometimes given as communications from God to individuals in private experiences and at other times presented as the words of God spoken by human messengers who passed on to their audiences sayings that they had presumably received from God in such private experiences. In many cases it would be hard to decide just where God stopped speaking and the human author took over – and indeed meaningless and futile to try to do so. How could one distinguish between the more personal expressions of Paul's emotions and his more direct statements of what he believed to be divine revelation?

Against this background what do we make of the statement 'Hear the Word of God' which so often accompanies a public reading from some part of the Bible? Some Christians would say that the Bible *is* the Word of God in the sense that every word of it comes from God, while others would say that it simply *contains* the Word of God along with other, human words. At first glance, the latter view might seem the better founded. If we say, however, that the Bible is the Word of God, it would seem to follow that we are using the phrase 'Word of God' in at least two senses. It is the same kind of problem as when we talk about the 'presence' of God. There is a sense in which God is omnipresent; he is everywhere, and nobody can escape from his presence (Ps. 139:7–12). But people also talk about occasions when God was especially near to them or when God was not with them, and both of these ways of speaking are found in the Bible (Matt. 18:20; Judg. 16:20). In the same kind of way, when we speak of the words of the prophets as the Word of God, we mean that in these cases God spoke in a direct manner to and through the prophets; but if we want to say that the other parts of the Bible (such as the prophets' prayers addressed to God or the mistaken words of evil men) are the Word of God, then clearly we are using the term in a broader kind of way, similar to that in which we talk more broadly of the omnipresence of God in comparison with particular experiences of his presence.

The problem, then, is whether we are justified in speaking of the Bible as a whole in this broader sense as the Word of God. There are certainly good grounds for doing so. There is, to begin with, our own personal experience that it is not just through the narrowly prophetic parts of the Bible that we actually do hear the voice of God. It would be simple to gather testimonies from Christians to show that every *kind* of material in the Bible can serve as a vehicle for conveying the Word of God to them. However, it must also be admitted that some Christians would say that there are some *parts* of the Bible which do not speak to them. The question cannot be settled simply by appealing to the conflicting voices of Christian experience. We must return to a consideration of what the biblical writers themselves say.

First, there are passages in the New Testament which

represent God as speaking through people like David (e.g. Acts 4:25). In Matthew 19:5 the words of Genesis 2:24, which are apparently the narrator's comment on the creation of Eve, 'Therefore a man leaves his father and his mother and cleaves to his wife, and they become one flesh', are attributed directly to God. These instances could be multiplied, so much so that B. B. Warfield was able to argue that the phrases 'it says', 'Scripture says' and 'God says' are virtually indistinguishable in meaning (*The Inspiration and Authority of the Bible*, London, 1951, pp. 299–348). His argument is broadly sound. There is a consensus of usage in the New Testament which shows that passages from the Old Testament generally were regarded as stemming ultimately from God. This is true not only of passages which might reasonably be regarded as 'prophetic' in the sense that they give words of God uttered through prophets, but also of other passages whose prophetic character is not obvious, such as Genesis 2:24.

A second point is that the New Testament writers regard the statements in the Old Testament as having unquestioned authority. They do not doubt that the prophetic messages really came from God. They accept the historical accounts and the wise sayings. It would not, in fact, have occurred to them to doubt them, since they shared this belief with their fellow-Jews. Now of course it might be objected that this last point weakens the argument; it could be said that the New Testament writers had not thought about the matter for themselves and simply took over existing Jewish attitudes without really discussing the point. But this argument will not in fact work.

On the one hand, the early Christians did think a lot about the Old Testament. They gave a new meaning to many passages in it, or rather they saw a new meaning in them as a result of their conviction that the Old Testament pointed forward to the coming of Jesus and the creation of the Church. There were lively debates regarding the interpretation of the Old Testament, and Christians asserted its authoritative backing for their own understanding of the significance of Jesus.

On the other hand, the early Christians soon came to see that certain parts of the Old Testament law were no longer valid for them now that the Messiah had come. It was no longer necessary to be circumcised to belong to the people of God. The teaching about making various kinds of sacrifices and about observing distinctions between clean and unclean foods was regarded as completely obsolete for Christians, whether they were Jews or Gentiles. Yet it was never suggested that such teaching had not come from God. Rather, what God had said in the past was now superseded by a fresh revelation of himself through Jesus Christ.

There was, then, this tension between those parts of the Old Testament which were still valid for Christians, especially the prophecies that were now being fulfilled and those statements of God's will which were still binding, and those parts which had lost their validity in the light of the new revelation in Jesus Christ. It would have been easy for Christians to suggest that some parts of the Old Testament were not the Word of God. But they did not do so. They maintained their belief in the divine origin of the Old Testament Scriptures while recognising that what was authoritative and valid for the people of God before the coming of Jesus was not necessarily so after his coming. The point is that the early Christians were confronted by the problem of the status of the Old Testament as the Word of God, and they affirmed their acceptance of it as such while recognising that some aspects of its teaching were no longer binding upon them, but were given for the people of Israel in an earlier dispensation.

There is a third point in our consideration of what the biblical writers themselves say on this subject. These general observations are confirmed by two specific passages in which the character of the Old Testament is described, namely 2 Peter 1:20 f. and 2 Timothy 3:16. These statements occur in letters which are traditionally attributed to Peter and Paul respectively. However, there is a strong body of scholarly opinion which holds that various features in the letters militate against this ascription and that the true authors are unknown. If this opinion is a correct one, it does not affect in any way the point which we are about to make, since our concern at present is simply to see what is said anywhere in the New Testament about the Old Testament. In other words, the objection which is sometimes made against using these passages on the grounds that their authorship is in doubt is irrelevant. Whether or not Peter and Paul wrote these passages, they represent statements by early Christians showing how they regarded the Old Testament.

The first passage tells us that 'no prophecy of scripture is a matter of one's own interpretation, because no prophecy ever came by the impulse of man, but men moved by the Holy Spirit spoke from God'. The point of this statement is to warn against individualistic, human interpretations of prophecy. The true interpretation of prophecy must come, it is implied, from the Spirit of God, since the prophecies were originally spoken by the Spirit. Prophecy was not a matter of the prophet deciding what he wanted to say; the prophets were men consecrated to the service of God, and they were impelled by the Holy Spirit so that what they said came from God. This of course does not mean that the prophets were merely passive in the process or that their natural faculties were superseded through some kind of ecstatic experience. Moreover, it should be noted that what is said here applies strictly only to prophetic statements which need interpretation, and it does not necessarily apply to the whole of the Old Testament.

The second passage states that 'all scripture is inspired by God and profitable for teaching, for reproof, for correction, and for training in righteousness'. It is also possible to translate the first part of this statement as 'every scripture inspired by God is also profitable . . .', and some scholars have taken this to mean that there might be some other scriptures which were not inspired by God. This suggestion can be confidently rejected, since no New Testament writer would have conceived of the possibility of a book being classified as Scripture and yet as not being inspired by God. Whichever translation we adopt – and the former is in any case the more probable – the point is that every part of Scripture is profitable for its divinely-intended purposes in virtue of its divine inspiration. The word translated 'inspired' is literally 'God-breathed', a rare word which is used of wisdom or dreams as having their source in God. The writings of the Old Testament as a whole are thus regarded as having a divine origin, although the precise relationship between their divine origin and their human composition is not explained here.

It should perhaps be commented that when the New Testament writers talk about 'the Scriptures' they are referring to the Old Testament as we know it in substantially its present form. The gathering together of the books of the Old Testament and the recognition of them as Scripture was virtually complete by the first century A.D. We know that the law, the prophets and the writings existed as the three parts of the Jewish Scriptures by the second century B.C.; some doubt remained about the inclusion of one or two minor books among the 'writings', but in all essentials the concept that certain books were to be regarded as Scripture, and the collection of the books that make up the Jewish Scriptures, our Old Testament, were in existence in the first century. The books known to Protestants as the Apocrypha of the Old Testament and to Roman Catholics as the Deuterocanonical Books were not part of the Jewish Scriptures. The Jews also treasured various unwritten 'traditions of the elders' (Mark 7:5) as being of equal authority with the written Scriptures, but these were never accepted by Jesus and his followers (Mark 7:8, 13). (See further R. T. Beckwith, 'Canon of the Old Testament', in *The Illustrated Bible Dictionary*, Leicester, 1980, I, pp. 235–239.)

So far we have been looking at what the New Testament writers have to say about the Old Testament. But what about the attitude of Jesus himself? His attitude is particularly important. Whatever authority we may be prepared to give to the New Testament writers at this stage when we have been simply gathering together what they said, we shall presumably be prepared to give at least some weight to the statements of Jesus if we claim to be his disciples, and we shall also be anxious to know whether the New Testament writers themselves were in agreement with his teaching.

Here we are faced by something of a problem in that many scholars query whether the Gospels give a historically accurate account of what Jesus actually taught. Obviously at this point in our enquiry it is not possible for us to say, 'Since the Gospels are the Word of God, therefore their accounts of what Jesus said must be accurate.' That would be to argue in a circle. We must be prepared, at least for the moment, to look at the Gospels as we would look at any other ancient documents and assess their historical reliability by the usual methods applied in such cases. Many scholars would treat the account of the teaching of Jesus given in John with considerable historical reserve, since it gives a very distinctive picture of Jesus when compared with the mutually similar accounts in the other three Gospels; they would argue that the teaching of the Evangelist and of Jesus have been so fused together that it is hard to be sure just exactly what Jesus said. With regard to the other three Gospels, however, we can be much more confident, so far as historical argument can take us, that the picture of Jesus is substantially reliable, and we can use them with considerable confidence as historical sources. (Here I may perhaps be permitted to refer to my book, *I Believe in the Historical Jesus*, London, 1977.) Opinions vary among scholars regarding whether we have the actual words of Jesus in the various accounts of what he said; it would not be surprising if writers telling the story some thirty or more years after his death should give the substance of what he said rather than his exact utterances word for word. At the very least, however, it can be said that the Gospels give us the impression which Jesus made on his followers, and, when we bear in mind the depth of their devotion to him, it would be extremely unlikely that their accounts of him should differ markedly from the reality. We can be confident that the first three Gospels at any rate give us a picture of Jesus that cannot be far removed from reality; and even if scholars are not equally confident about the fourth Gospel, its contents still mirror the profound impression made by Jesus on its writer.

When we look at the Gospels to see how Jesus regarded the

Old Testament, there is in fact ample evidence to show that he had the same attitude as his disciples. He settled disputes by appeals to its authoritative teaching, and he regarded certain of its prophecies as being confirmed by being fulfilled in his own career. It is true that he went beyond its teaching in various respects, as when he showed that the law of Moses did not go far enough as a guide for the lives of his disciples (Matt. 5), and when he implicitly did away with the laws regarding clean and unclean food as no longer applicable to his disciples (Mark 7:19), but in all major respects his teaching could be shown to be in line with its essential spirit. The teaching of Jesus shows a mind that was nourished on the Scriptures and which drew its inspiration from them. Without going into details (for which see R. T. France, *Jesus and the Old Testament*, London, 1971) we can affirm that Jesus accepted the Old Testament Scriptures as the Word of God.

To be sure, any other conclusion would be extremely surprising when we bear in mind the attitude of the followers of Jesus. They could very easily have dealt with some of the arguments pitted against them by the Jews if they had simply denied the authority of the Old Testament. In fact they did not do so, and it is highly probable that they were simply following the example of Jesus in this matter. If Jesus had rejected the authority of the Old Testament in any way, it is surely extremely likely that he would have influenced his followers to adopt the same attitude.

So far we have looked at the attitude of the New Testament writers and of Jesus to the Old Testament, a matter concerning which there is no shortage of evidence. It is less easy to comment on how the New Testament writers regarded their own writings. They do not have much to say about themselves or their colleagues. Yet indirectly some of them do show a consciousness that they were not producing merely human documents. Thus when Paul begins his letters, he normally stresses his position in the Church as an apostle or servant of Jesus Christ. By so doing he lays claim to some authority over the churches to which he writes, and we should not underestimate the force of this claim. For Paul the apostles were the leading figures in the ministry of the Church (1 Cor. 12:28), more important even than the prophets who occupied a vital position as the bearers of God's revelation to the Church. The early Church believed that prophecy had come to life again in its midst, and that God had new things to reveal to his people. For Paul, the apostle occupied an even higher place than the prophet, and there can be no doubt that he regarded his own letters, highly personal documents though they are, as being written as part of the exercise of his apostolic ministry. He was not averse to making statements in them to which he himself would have attached the authority of God (e.g. 1 Cor. 7:25, 40). This point is underlined in Ephesians 2:20, 3:5 where the place of the apostles and prophets as the foundation of the Church is stressed. A similar position to that of Paul is claimed by the authors of 1 and 2 Peter, James and Jude. The author of Revelation expressly entitles his work as a 'revelation' which God had shown to him, and his understanding of its character as an inviolable prophecy is seen in the strict warning he gives in 22:18 f.

So far as the Gospels are concerned, it is interesting that Luke in particular adopted an Old Testament style of narration which has led to the view that he consciously felt that he was writing an account of God's great acts for human salvation of the same kind as he found in the Old Testament. The Evangelists incorporated in their works traditions about Jesus which were regarded as authoritative in the Church. If what Jesus said was authoritative (1 Cor. 9:14), so too were accounts of what he said and did (1 Cor. 11:23–25).

There was probably, therefore, a certain sense that the books of the New Testament were not simply human accounts and letters, although it would be wrong to suggest that the writers felt conscious that they were writing Scripture. Nevertheless, John's Gospel contains the promise that the Holy Spirit would bring to the remembrance of the disciples all that Jesus had said (John 14:26), and it is likely that the author believed that God was doing precisely this through him, helping him to remember and express afresh the significance of what Jesus had said for new generations of believers.

29

Finally, we have the stage where the author of 2 Peter can place the writings of Paul alongside what he calls 'the other scriptures', and this implicitly affirm their status as Scripture (2 Pet. 3:16). All this suggests a growing realisation that the New Testament writers were composing works comparable in character and authority with the Old Testament Scriptures.

We have now gathered together in brief outline the essential elements in 'what the Bible says about itself'. The evidence is obviously fragmentary and unsystematic, which is not surprising when we consider the long period of time over which the books of the Bible were written by many authors. But we have been able to trace a general consciousness that the biblical writings were authoritative expressions of the Word of God, whether in the specific sense of purporting to be records of what God had said to the prophets or in the more general sense of being works inspired by his Spirit.

2

WHAT DO WE MEAN BY 'INSPIRATION'?

When we talk about the nature of the Bible as a book through which God reveals himself to us, words and phrases like 'Word of God', 'inspiration' and 'authority' find their way into our discussion. Having seen in the previous chapter that the Old Testament Scriptures are described as 'inspired' in 2 Timothy, we must now try to come to grips with this term, since it may be the key to understanding what it is that makes the Bible into a source of divine revelation. Various attempts have been made to understand inspiration, and it will be helpful to look at them in turn.

1. Perhaps the most familiar way of expressing the nature of inspiration is in terms of the experience of the prophets. A prophet was often conscious of receiving a divine message through a dream or vision or inward voice, and this divine message could be put into words. Then what he heard from God was usually spoken by the prophet to the people for whom it was intended, and eventually it was written down for wider circulation, either by the prophet himself or by his hearers or followers. A good deal of biblical material is presented as originating in this kind of way. It is then tempting to go further and claim that the rest of the biblical material is to be understood as having been communicated in the same way; God inspired the biblical writers in general in the same way as he inspired the prophets. Thus the whole Bible can be understood as the product of prophetic inspiration.

Since the prophets often give the impression that God's message came to them in a verbal form, and that they then repeated it aloud or wrote it down word for word, it would not be unfair to describe the process envisaged as one of dictation. God told the prophets precisely what he wanted them to say on his behalf, and they then passed the message on more or less verbatim, though perhaps with some individual freedom of expression. If we then go on to explain the rest of the biblical material by means of this analogy, we would be saying that the biblical writers received what to say by dictation from God himself.

This type of 'prophetic' understanding of divine inspiration as a form of dictation is probably held, at least unconsciously, by a number of Christians. How, for example, did the author of Genesis know what had happened in the Garden of Eden – assuming that what he has given us is a historical report of the matter? If we do not hold the view seriously advanced by some writers that the story of Adam and Eve was handed down by word of mouth from one generation of their descendants to another, then we must suppose that God dictated the story directly to the author of Genesis. Likewise, when Luke tells us about conversations held behind closed doors (e.g. Acts 26:30–32), then we must assume that, if nobody leaked the information to him, God must have told him precisely what was said.

Although the 'prophetic' or 'dictation' theory of the composition of the Bible has sometimes been held by theologians, it has no support from modern scholars. It is open to a number of cogent objections. Basically it does not correspond to the facts in the Bible itself. While it is true that the prophets claimed to hear God speaking to them, and then proclaimed his Word, this was not how the other writers pictured themselves as working. They used human sources of information and worked in the usual sorts of ways practised by writers. They did not function as divine tape-recorders or word-processors, instruments controlled entirely by their users. So Luke tells us that other people before him had attempted to write the story of Jesus, and the implication of his statement (Luke 1:1–4), which is confirmed by a study of his gospel, is that he consulted their works and made use of them in compiling his own. Paul clearly wrote his letters as spontaneous compositions, expressive of his own thoughts and ideas. Various writers are depicted as asking God questions (even the prophets do so), and it hardly seems probable that God dictated their own personal feelings and expressions to them. The whole tenor of what the biblical writers say about themselves is that they composed their books by using normal human mental processes.

Sometimes the biblical writers quote secular sources, such as Persian archives (e.g. Ezra 7:11–26). It is impossible to think of such sources as being dictated by God, and it is farcical to suggest that they became inspired when they were copied out by Ezra.

What in effect has happened is that the biblical writers have been depersonalised – and indeed God himself has been depersonalised, since he no longer acts as a person dealing with persons, but as a workman using a tool. The Bible is no longer regarded as in any real sense a human book; it is simply a heavenly telegram. In short, the theory not only does not correspond to what the biblical writers tell us about themselves; it also leads to a false view of God's relationships with human persons.

One further point must be made. The theory assumes that whenever a prophet received a message from God it came to him in the form of a message which he heard, so that all that he had to do was to repeat God's words. There is no need to doubt that this was the experience of the prophets on occasion. What is dubious is whether all divine messages came in this way. For example, when Jeremiah went down to the potter's house and there heard the Lord drawing a message from what the potter did with the clay (Jer. 18:1–11), it is an open question whether he actually heard the voice of God, or rather came to a personal conviction about God's purpose for his people as he meditated on what the potter was doing and then realised that this conviction was God's Word for the people. Since the messages which the prophets proclaimed as the words of God are couched in their own distinctive literary styles rather than being in one uniform 'divine' style, it seems quite clear that even in the case of the prophets the theory of direct dictation is not universally applicable.

2. At the opposite extreme from this understanding of the Bible is the view that the Scriptures are nothing more than the work of men of remarkable religious insight with the ability to express themselves in eloquent language. When the Speaker of the House of Commons read the lesson from 1 Corinthians 13 at the wedding of the Prince and Princess of Wales, several members of the public, whose familiarity with the Bible left something to be desired, wrote in and asked for a copy of the script of his speech, so eloquent and moving had they found it. The passage which he read is a moving piece of prose which strikes home by its poetic quality and its insight into ultimate values. Its writer shows the same qualities as we find in great poets and novelists who are artists in words, capable of recognising profound truths and expressing them in a memorable and impressive manner. May it not be said, then, that the inspiration of the Bible lies in this quality of expressing ultimate truths as they have been recognised and given verbal form by men of genius?

It would be false to deny the presence of such elements in the Bible; it can be recognised to be among the great literature of the world. But obviously this is not true of it all. One cannot attribute this level of religious or literary insight to the composer of some of the genealogies or lists of legal regulations in the Old Testament. No doubt the upholders of such a view of the Bible would cheerfully admit this. They would point out that the inspiration of the Bible is patchy; some of its contents are pedestrian in character, or even false in their understanding of God and mankind.

One difficulty with this view is that Christians find that they can hear God speaking through the uninspiring parts of the Bible as well as the inspiring. A theory which confines inspiration to a few purple passages is unable to cope with the Bible as a whole.

Much more serious is the objection that this view leaves no room for the factor that inspired the previous view, the presence of 'prophetic' material in the Bible. It makes the Bible into a record of human insights of varying quality, a book no different in kind from other books. Maybe this is how the Bible appears to non-Christians. It is a totally inadequate view for Christian believers who accept that divine revelation is something more than human insight. Nevertheless, before we dismiss this view as a complete failure to grasp the reality of divine inspiration, we should observe that it does draw our attention to a very real human quality of the Bible as literature. Our total view of the Bible must take this human side into account.

3. A different kind of view is that the Bible is to be understood as a witness to divine revelation rather than as revelation itself. The 'religious insight' view of the Bible is generally coupled with an understanding of religion as being itself the exercise of what we may call the human religious consciousness. It leaves no room for divine acts of revelation. The view now under discussion, however, attaches great importance to the events in the history of Israel, the career of Jesus and the development of the Church which can be regarded as showing the activity of God. The Bible is to be seen as the record of such events, and therein lies its unique importance. No particular inspiration was required in order to write it, other than the kind of pressure that arises out of a compelling experience. For instance, a person witnessing a devastating battle may be moved to describe it in such a way that the futility and cruelty of war become very obvious. So, too, the person who has seen Jesus or experienced the coming of the Spirit may be moved to testify to what has happened.

Some of the objections to this view have already been discussed in the Introduction; there we tried to show that divine revelation in events needs to be accompanied by an interpretation which is itself part of the process of revelation. When the Israelites crossed the Red Sea without getting their feet wet, their ability to do so might well have been simply due to a freak of nature; it required a religious leader to interpret the event as an act of God and to do so with authority. Further, it is through the biblical account that the crossing of the Red Sea continues to be understood as a divine act by successive generations of believers. In other words, granted that the

Bible is a witness to acts of revelation, its character as witness makes it a part of the total act of divine revelation, and we still need to ask what it is that gives it this character of divine revelation. It is not enough to say that it is merely human testimony to what happened; something more than human testimony is necessary if the Bible is to continue to function as a means of revelation.

A second objection to this view is that a good deal of the Bible cannot be explained as witness to revelatory events. There is much detailed expression of the will of God as given in the Old Testament laws or the New Testament exhortations and teaching. It is stretching the point unduly to say that all this is merely human response to revelatory events or that it is merely the record of revelation as opposed to revelation itself. Much of the Bible claims to be revelation itself.

4. The views that we have been considering all deal with the nature of the composition of the Bible. A different type of theory holds that the Bible may be no different from other books as regards its composition, but it is different in that the Holy Spirit can use it and make it a means of revelation by speaking through it to particular individuals and communities. The Bible *becomes* revelation through the continuing inspiration of the Spirit.

The main proponent of this view of inspiration is the theologian Karl Barth. He links it closely with an acceptance of the view that the Bible is a witness to God's original act of revelation. The Bible is then able to become a source of revelation to us as the Spirit inspires it in our contemporary situation. In this way Barth can speak of the Bible as being the Word of God. It would be wrong to dissociate this second part of Barth's doctrine from the first part. He wants to emphasise that the Bible is indeed different in content from other books in that it is the witness to God's revelation in Jesus Christ, but he appears to want to deny that the Bible differs from other books as regards the manner of its original composition. To be sure, he is perhaps not wholly consistent on this point, as more than one commentator on his work has observed. He wants to guard against the dangers of thinking that the Holy Spirit is somehow shut up in a Bible that can remain a dead letter to unbelievers. This danger is met by his insistence that it needs the Spirit today to reveal the Word of God through Scripture to the reader. But those who hold that the Spirit inspired the original composition of Scripture also would insist that the same Spirit continues to illumine the text so that it comes alive for its readers. The weakness in Barth's position is that in his insistence on the need for *illumination now* he tends to deny *inspiration then*, although the two activities of the Spirit are surely complementary and in no way exclusive of each other. It is very doubtful whether Barth's view does justice to that very character of the Bible as inspired Scripture which makes it possible for the Spirit to continue to witness through its words to the Word of God which it embodies. It has been suggested that Barth himself in his later years may have come to some recognition of this weakness in his view of the Bible, but we have to go by what he actually wrote, and it must be confessed that it is not entirely satisfactory.

5. The view of the Bible which we have just discussed is more concerned with how it functions today as the Word of God than with its original composition. Two recent attempts to wrestle with the latter question may be briefly noted as typical of current approaches. The first is *The Inspiration of Scripture* (Philadelphia, 1980) by Paul J. Achtemeier, who stands over against the so-called liberal and conservative camps in trying to find a view of Scripture that does justice to the strengths of both sides and avoids the weaknesses of both. The weakness of the liberal view is that it views the Bible too much in terms of human religious genius and progressive discovery of the truth (see view 2. above) and ignores the elements of its inspiration and authority which are rightly stressed by conservative scholars. The weakness of the conservative view is that it sees the Bible too one-sidedly as a book produced directly by the Spirit of God and ignores the elements of human composition – and human fallibility – in the Bible. These concerns, of course, lay at the root of Barth's position;

37

he wanted to be able to say that the Bible is the Word of God and yet to allow for its character as a fully human composition, and he did so by playing down the place of the Spirit in its composition. Achtemeier, however, wants to insist on the very real activity of the Spirit in the composition of the Bible, and he draws attention to the complex nature of the process of composition of the Bible. It is in this area of composition that he finds the place for inspiration. The composition of the biblical books arises out of the coming together of traditions regarding what God has done, the situation faced by the believing community in which it tries to understand and apply its inherited traditions, and the activity of 'respondents' who take up the traditions and reformulate them in specific situations, thus producing the Scriptures. It is in this process that the Spirit is at work, not just at the moment of final composition but in the whole history of the formulation of the traditions, and again not just in the process of composition but in the whole process of Scripture being read and interpreted today.

This is a helpful and positive approach which seeks to do justice to the Bible's own testimony to the activity of the Spirit in its composition, and which recognises the complexity of that process. There are insights here which must certainly be incorporated in any attempt to reach an understanding of the nature of inspiration. The weakness of the view is that it locates inspiration as an activity in the process of composition of the Bible and does not really tackle the issue of the inspiredness of the resulting book. Achtemeier does not consider the actual character of the Bible as an inspired book sufficiently clearly. He seems to want to relate the work of the Spirit today to assurance of the truth of the particular contents of the Bible rather than to assurance that the Bible as such is the source of truth. There is a gap between the process of inspiration and the text of the Bible which causes some disquiet, particularly when we remember that according to 2 Timothy it is the Scriptures which are inspired rather than the process of composition.

6. The other recent contribution to the debate which we shall briefly mention is *The Divine Inspiration of Holy Scripture* (Oxford, 1981) by William J. Abraham. This book is written from within the evangelical tradition by a writer who has problems with traditional conservative concepts of infallibility and inerrancy. He argues that insufficient attention has been paid to the meaning of the term 'inspiration'. In ordinary usage the term is used of the way in which, for example, a good teacher will 'inspire' his pupils to produce good work which would not have been possible for them without his creative guidance, but which nevertheless remains their own proper and distinctive work. One may then apply this concept to the way in which God used his revelatory and saving acts for his people, and his personal dealings with individuals, to lead them to write and collect together the books of the Bible; and since God himself is omniscient and infallible and consciously initiated this process, it follows that the resulting product will be true and reliable, although not necessarily infallible in every particular.

This view of inspiration is broader than that of God 'dictating the contents of the Bible', the view against which Abraham is to some extent reacting. It is also in some ways more attractive. One of the worst university teachers I ever had was a lecturer who used to dictate her lecture notes to the class (yes, at dictation speed) rather than stimulate us to make our own notes of what we saw as important in the light of her teaching and to incorporate our own personal touch in them. Such dictation is not true teaching; it is reminiscent of the old quip that a lecture is a process whereby information passes from the lecture notes of the professor to the note books of the students without passing through the minds of either. True teaching respects and cultivates the minds of the taught, recognising that the latter must be trained to make their own contribution to their acquisition of knowledge.

It can be objected, of course, that divine revelation ought to be a one-way process of dictation since the facts at issue are too important to be transmitted in any other way to purely receptive individuals, and that a method of transmission in which the human recipients have any significant contribution to make is altogether too loose and uncontrolled to be the means for the communication of God's truth. However, if the human minds are those of receptive believers, in whom the Spirit is at work, the process is surely sufficiently under divine control and guidance. Whether Abraham would want to say this is uncertain; one gains the impression that he is thinking more of the powerful initiating impulse of God on the biblical writers rather than of total divine control of the process. Again, therefore, as in the case of Achtemeier, one may question whether there is something of a gap between the inspiration of the biblical writers and the inspiration of the writings themselves.

Abraham's suggestion is open to a further criticism in that it rightly appeals to the meaning of the biblical word 'inspired', but that it begins from the English usage of the concept rather than from the Greek word and its usage. It is not self-evident that the field of meaning and usage of the English concept is identical with that of the Greek word, and the evidence is rather against it.

7. We turn, finally, to consider the type of understanding of inspiration associated with modern conservative writers. The 'classical' treatments are those of B. B. Warfield, *The Inspiration and Authority of the Bible* (London, 1951), and James Orr, *Revelation and Inspiration* (London, 1910), both of which still repay study. Their views have given rise to a massive literature in the past few years, out of which Clark H. Pinnock's book, *Biblical Revelation* (Chicago, 1971), deserves mention as an important North American contribution. For our present purpose, however, the best starting point is given by the English writer J. I. Packer in his *Fundamentalism and the Word of God* (London, 1958), and *God has Spoken* (London, 1979).

Packer's proposal is that we should think of inspiration in terms of what he calls the 'concursive action' of the Spirit of God in the composition of the Bible. An analogy may help to clarify the idea. If we try to explain the idea of God's creation and providence in the universe, we can describe what happens on two levels. On the one level, we can explain much, though not necessarily all, of what happens in terms of ordinary cause and effect. This is the method followed in scientific investigations of the origins and working of the universe, and it is a perfectly legitimate and fruitful method. On the other level, we can explain creation as the act of God and we can also postulate his continuing providential care of the world. For the most part these two explanations are complementary. We are looking at the same phenomena from two different points of view; it is not a case of explaining some things scientifically and other things (a diminishing number) by recourse to what has been called the theory of the 'God of the gaps'. Scientist and theologian are asking two different, complementary questions. If the scientist is a Christian, he accepts the divine origin of the universe and also the legitimacy of understanding it on the level of natural cause and effect.

There will, of course, be supernatural events in the universe which cannot be accounted for in natural terms, such as the incarnation and resurrection of the Son of God, and there will also be natural events which by reason of their timing or other characteristics can be understood by the believer as acts of God, such as the return of the Jewish exiles from Babylon or the destruction of Jerusalem by the Romans in A.D. 70. In some cases it may be difficult to draw a firm line between what is supernatural and what is natural. Nevertheless, for the most part one can say that there are two complementary levels of explanation of phenomena in the natural universe, and that care must be taken not to confuse the types of explanation or to assume that only one of them will be applicable in any given situation.

Against this background let us briefly look at the problems raised by the origin of the universe. On the one hand, scientific explanation can take us so far in understanding, but only so far. We cannot go back right up to the 'moment' of creation and look at what was happening 'before' it (if it is legitimate to talk in these terms at all). On the other hand, we cannot describe or explain creation from a theological point

41

of view except by using the language of metaphor and symbol. We have to use two different sorts of language, religious language and scientific language, and we cannot bring these together in a single description of creation. For it is impossible to bring together divine causation and natural causation and show how they are related to each other. The reason for this is that as finite human beings we cannot in principle understand how the finite and the infinite are related to each other. All that we can do is, on the one hand, to let scientific explanation take us as far as it can and recognise that there are limits to its powers of explanation, and, on the other hand, to state our belief in the action of God in metaphorical and symbolical terms, recognising that we cannot describe God's action in literal terms.

The point of this analogy, then, is that we can describe events from two angles in complementary ways, and that we have to recognise the dangers of confusing the two types of explanation.

We can now move on to suggest that the composition of the Bible can be understood in the same kind of way. On a human level we can describe its composition in terms of the various oral and literary processes that lay behind it – the collection of information from witnesses, the use of written sources, the writing up and editing of such information, the composition of spontaneous letters, the committing to writing of prophetic messages, the collecting of the various documents together, and so on. At the same time, however, on the divine level we can assert that the Spirit, who moved on the face of the waters at Creation (Gen. 1:2), was active in the whole process so that the Bible can be regarded as both the words of men and the Word of God. This activity of the Spirit can be described as 'concursive' with the human activities through which the Bible was written.

This hypothesis does full justice to the claim in 2 Timothy 3:16 that all Scripture is God-breathed; it is the product of the inspiration of the Spirit of God. What is being asserted is the activity of God throughout the whole of the process so that the whole of the product ultimately comes from him. At the same time it allows for the activity of the Spirit in special ways within the process without requiring that we understand all of the Spirit's working in one and the same way. Just as in the case of the creation and preservation of the universe we can observe points where God intervened in unusual ways for specific purposes, so too we can say that alongside and within this general concursive action of the Spirit in inspiring normal human forms of composition in the biblical books, we can trace special actions of the Spirit in bringing special revelations to prophets and apostles. For example, in the case of Jeremiah we can recognise the special action of God in revealing specific messages to the prophet and a more general, but equally important, activity of the Spirit in the composition of the historical reports in the book.

Equally, this hypothesis does full justice to the human factors in the composition of the Bible. It avoids any suspicion that the books of the Bible were dictated to their human authors so that they had no real part in their composition. The Jewish writer Philo held a view of inspiration according to which the writers of the Old Testament were like musical instruments on which God played his own tunes. The inspired writer, he commented, is 'the vocal instrument of God, smitten and played by his invisible hand'. Here the action of the human personality is suspended and plays little or no part in the composition of Scripture. There is no suggestion of this kind in the view that we are propounding. It takes the human circumstances of composition of the Bible seriously.

In particular we are able to cope with the very varied character of the different parts of the Bible and the complex character of its composition. Not only is the Bible a collection of separate books, written by many different individuals over a long period of time; it also includes, even within the confines of any one book, a vast variety of material, ranging from records of revelatory experiences to the quotation of secular documents. The composition of the various books was also in many cases a long process involving not just single writers but large groups of people who handed down traditions and helped to produce written materials that were ultimately

43

incorporated into the books that we have; for example, Joshua 10:13 and 2 Samuel 1:18 both note that the biblical writers are quoting from the 'Book of Jashar'. The old idea of God individually dictating the contents of the various books directly to their authors failed to take this process of composition into account, and this is one of the reasons why the doctrine of inspiration seemed incredible to many scholars. The trouble was that the doctrine had been expressed in terms of a specific theory of the human composition of Scripture: when the latter was felt to be unacceptable, it was natural to assume that the former was also untenable. Once the doctrine of inspiration is freed from an untenable view of the composition of the Bible, it becomes possible to reinstate it in a more secure form. For it is obvious that the concursive action of the Spirit is not tied to one particular understanding of how the books of the Bible were written. Rather, God was at work in the whole process of composition.

In view of what we said earlier about the analogy with creation, our hypothesis does not explain *how* inspiration took place. Our human minds cannot bring together 'theological' explanations in terms of divine causation and the work of the Spirit and 'natural' explanations in terms of historical and literary processes. We cannot, to use another relevant example, understand the relationship between the sanctifying work of the Spirit in our own lives and the activity of our own wills. The doctrine of inspiration is a declaration that the Scriptures have their origin in God; it is not and cannot be an explanation of how God brought them into being.

One particular analogy which has sometimes been used to explain the character of inspiration is that of the person of Jesus Christ. The union of the divine and the human in Jesus so that he was both fully the Son of God and perfect man has been used to throw light on the nature of Scripture as being simultaneously God's Word and man's words. I have refrained from discussing this point in detail since I am not sure how helpful it is. The fact is that the problems of understanding the person of Christ are so great that it is far from obvious that a discussion of this point can help to clarify the doctrine of

Scripture. Different conclusions have been drawn from the analogy by scholars of varying viewpoints. Again, it is not clear whether the analogy is properly applied to the human agents through whom God was active in the composition of Scripture or to the actual product of his inspiration. What the doctrine of the incarnation does do is to show that a real activity of God in the person of his Son is possible in the human dimension, and thus to make it all the more credible that God could work in other human beings to communicate his Word in human words. But the differences between the incarnation of the eternal Word in the person of Jesus and the divine composition of Scripture through human authors are so considerable that it is perhaps wiser not to hang a doctrine of Scripture on conclusions drawn from an analogy.

Finally, we must ask whether the doctrine of inspiration, as we have outlined it, is true. So far all that we have done is to take up what the Biblical writers say about their writings and to frame a hypothesis which will account for their statements. One important question, therefore, is whether our hypothesis is more satisfactory than the other proposed explanations. We have seen that none of the various suggestions was completely satisfactory, although we recognised that each of them attempted to do justice to some particular aspects of the character of the Bible. It is for the reader to judge whether our hypothesis is free from the shortcomings and difficulties which we encountered in the other views.

A second question is whether what the biblical writers say about their work, and the hypothesis which we have constructed, are open to any objections based on the actual character of the Bible. For example, if the Bible contained palpably false statements, then this would be a serious objection to accepting a doctrine of inspiration and revelation. We shall, therefore, need to look very closely at this area in later parts of this book. Meanwhile, however, we can make an important general point. If we revert for a moment to the analogy with creation, we may note that some features of the universe, such as the indications of design and pattern which we can see in it, point to the probability of a Creator. At the same time, other features, such as the presence of suffering and pain, may be regarded as evidence against the existence of a Creator. Ultimately, acceptance of the existence of a Creator is a matter of faith and not of proof; it involves a step of faith that not everybody is prepared to take and which some people emphatically refuse to take. In the same way, various features of the Bible, such as its lofty teaching or the way in which some of its prophecies have been fulfilled, may act as pointers to belief in its divine inspiration, while other features of the Bible, such as unresolved historical problems or ethically questionable teaching, may appear to point in a different direction. In the end, therefore, it is a matter of faith whether we accept the hypothesis of the divine inspiration of Scripture. Or, to put the matter from a complementary angle, it is the result of the working of the Spirit in our minds to initiate and sustain faith.

There is, to be sure, one particular ground which may be decisive. It can be argued that our acceptance of the Bible as the Word of God rests upon the authoritative teaching of Jesus; if we accept him as our Lord, then we shall accept and share his attitude to the Scriptures. There are, however, two problems here. The first is the factual one of whether Jesus held a view of the Old Testament which would substantiate a belief in its divine inspiration. Here opinions will no doubt differ, and we can only state our view that Jesus did regard the Old Testament Scriptures as the inspired Word of God. The second problem is that our acceptance of Jesus as an authoritative guide on anything is also a matter of faith, so that the question of faith is simply pushed back one stage. That is to say, in the end our acceptance of the Bible as the inspired Word of God is a matter of faith and not of rational proof. It is bound up with our attitude towards Jesus and the teaching of the apostles and prophets.

The balance between these two factors of rational argument and faith generated by the Spirit is well expressed in the classic words of the Westminster Confession:

We may be moved and induced by the testimony of the

Church to an high and revered esteem of the holy scripture, and the heavenliness of the matter, the efficacy of the doctrine, the majesty of the style, the consent of all the parts, the scope of the whole (which is to give all glory to God), the full discovery it makes of the only way of man's salvation, the many other incomparable excellencies, and the entire perfection thereof, are arguments whereby it doth abundantly evidence itself to be the word of God; yet, nothwithstanding, our full persuasion and assurance of the infallible truth, and divine authority thereof, is from the inward work of the Holy Spirit, bearing witness by and with the word in our hearts. (1:5)

3

WHAT ARE THE RESULTS OF INSPIRATION?

We saw in the previous chapter that there are various ways of understanding the nature of the Bible. All who believe that in some sense it reveals God to us have to find some explanation of how this takes place. We recognised that the Bible does contain what purport to be direct messages in words from God to men, but that we cannot understand the whole Bible as the result of divine dictation. Equally we saw that the Bible is not simply the fruit of human writers possessed of religious insight and the skill to put their insight into words. We considered the views, which often go together, that the Bible is a witness to God's acts of revelation and that through the present activity of the Spirit it can become the Word of God for people today, and we argued that this does not do justice to the fact that revelation comes in word as well as in deed and also to the fact that the biblical writers believed that the Spirit was operative in the actual composition of the books. We then discussed two recent views which attempt to break out of the current impasse, the one by broadening the locus of inspiration to cover the whole complex interplay of tradition, situation and respondent which led to the writing of the biblical books, and the other by understanding inspiration not in terms of divine dictation but in terms of the good teacher who guides his pupils to the truth. Both of these views are helpful, especially the first, but we argued that they leave something of a gap between the activity of God and the actual text of the biblical books. Finally, we took a fresh look at the concept of the concursive action of the Spirit, and suggested that this understanding of the way in which the Scriptures can be seen on one level as the work of the Spirit and on another level as the work of human authors does justice to what the biblical writers say about their compositions. We then argued that, if we are correct in seeing this as an explanation which makes good sense of the biblical evidence, then the question is whether we are prepared to take a step of faith and accept it as true. We admitted that we cannot prove it to be true, although we can suggest factors which may help to persuade us of its truth.

We must now go on to look at two related questions. The one consists in unpacking the idea of inspiration to see what it means to speak of the Bible as the inspired Word of God. The other is to see whether in this discussion we find ourselves up against any difficulties which would militate against this understanding of the nature of the Bible.

It is at this point that we run full tilt into the two types of attitude to the Bible which we encountered at the outset of our enquiry.

First of all, there is one group of Christians for whom the inspiration of the Bible is associated with its infallibility or, to use the word which is becoming increasingly fashionable, its inerrancy. The meanings of these two terms may not be immediately clear, and therefore it may be useful to quote the definitions of them in 'The Chicago Statement on Biblical Inerrancy':

Infallible signifies the quality of neither misleading nor being misled and so safeguards in categorical terms the truth that Holy Scripture is a sure, safe and reliable guide in all matters.

Similarly, *inerrant* signifies the quality of being free from all falsehood or mistakes and so safeguards the truth that Holy Scripture is entirely true and trustworthy in all its assertions.

The ordinary reader may find it hard to distinguish between the meanings of these two words even after reading these definitions, and it should be added that some writers would say that the words are essentially the same in meaning.

Christians who use these terms believe that because a

statement is made in the Bible, God's inspired Word, therefore it must be true and reliable. They also argue in defence of their belief that, since God is the God of truth, therefore whatever he says in the Bible must be true, and hence the Bible must be infallible and inerrant.

This statement raises its own problems. On the one hand, we have already underlined the fact that acceptance of the Bible as the inspired Word of God is a matter of faith. Therefore, the claim that what the Bible says is true cannot be anything else than a statement of faith, which may or may not be ultimately justified. On the other hand, we have to ask what effect the inspiration of the Bible has on its teaching. Does inspiration imply infallibility, and what exactly is meant by infallibility anyhow? This is the nub of the matter.

Then there is the other group of Christians who find that, however much they may believe that the Bible contains the Word of God, the Bible does contain errors and contradictions; thus for them there is an insuperable barrier to saying that the Bible is infallible or inerrant, and they find it hard, if not totally impossible, to understand the position of the first group of Christians. For them the actual characteristics of the Bible militate against its infallibility, and so they look for some other view of the inspiration of the Bible which will be free from this difficulty. They also point out that the first group see the Bible as essentially a divine book and ignore its human features.

The debate between these two points of view has not been altogether edifying. From the side of the second group of Christians there have come some sharp and vituperative attacks on what is sometimes dubbed 'fundamentalism' in a disparaging sense, i.e. the view which holds that absolute truth is to be found in some sacrosanct set of words whose teaching should be followed without any questioning. But equally, within the first group of Christians, there have been some harsh attacks on anybody within or without (but especially within) the group who dares to raise any doubts about the understanding of inspiration which has come to be traditional in the group. There is an intense fear that any restatement of the doctrine will lead to an abandonment of divine truth as revealed in the Bible and is the start of a gradual declension from the faith which can end only in error and heresy. If we can find a common area of agreement on which to base our discussion, it will be in the statement that we must endeavour to do justice to the actual teaching and character of the Bible; for the first group of Christians the Bible is the supreme authority, and for the latter group the aim of study is to understand the actual character of the Bible. If this is a fair assumption, then there may be some hope of fruitful discussion and progress in debate.

A helpful line is to suggest a shift of focus in approaching the question of the effects of inspiration. Contemporary defenders of a conservative understanding of the nature of the Bible argue that, if God is the God of truth, and if he is the ultimate author of the Bible, then it follows that all that is said in the Bible must be true. It is obvious that this would be a valid piece of reasoning if the Bible had in fact been dictated by God to his human scribes who reproduced his words exactly. We have seen, however, that this theory of inspiration is incompatible with what the biblical writers say about themselves. If we were to hold simply that the biblical writers made their own response to the divine revelation which came to them, then there would be room for inadequate and even mistaken response by them in their writings. In between these two extremes there lies the theory of B. B. Warfield and his followers. They interpret the effect of the concursive action of the Spirit to mean that, although God did not use the *method* of dictating his words to the biblical writers, the *effect* of inspiration was to *produce* the same result. Although the biblical writers wrote freely when the matter is considered on a human level, in fact they were unconsciously prepared and led by God to write exactly what he wished to be written. In a well-known passage, which incidentally shows that he was fully aware that the process of inspiration extended far backwards in time before the actual moment of writing each individual book, Warfield commented: 'If God wished to give His people a series of letters like Paul's, He prepared a Paul to write them, and the Paul He brought to the task was a Paul who spontaneously would write just such letters.' (*The Inspiration and Authority of the Bible*, London, 1951, p. 155).

Now the crucial point here is the concept of what God *wished* to be written. Our ideas of what *we* may have wished God to write may not be the same as what *he* may have wished to write. If we look once again at 2 Timothy 3:15 f. we find that the stated purpose of the Scriptures is to provide the instruction that leads to salvation through faith in Christ Jesus, and this is then detailed in terms of teaching, reproof, correction and training which enable the man of God to be fully equipped for every good work. The purpose of God in the composition of the Scriptures was to guide people to salvation and the associated way of life. From this statement we may surely conclude that God made the Bible all that it needs to be in order to achieve this purpose. It is in this sense that the word 'infallible' is properly applied to the Bible; it means that it is 'in itself a true and sufficient guide, which may be trusted implicitly', (this is the definition given in an early edition of *Evangelical Belief*, the official interpretation of the doctrinal basis of the Inter-Varsity Fellowship, now known as the Universities and Colleges Christian Fellowship). We may therefore suggest that 'infallible' means that the Bible is entirely trustworthy for the purposes for which God inspired it. It will be noted that this description applies to 'all Scriptures'.

The effect of drawing out the significance of inspiration in this way is to shift the focus of the discussion from the truth of the Bible to its adequacy for what God intends it to do. We have been led to take this step by our endeavour to expound correctly what is actually said in 2 Timothy 3:15 f. But when we do this, we shall find that it opens up the possibility of a fresh approach to the Bible which may prove to be illuminating.

Accordingly, we may note that a concern for the truth of the Bible in every part may be too narrow and even inappropriate. Properly speaking, 'true' and its opposite, 'false', are qualities of statements or propositions which convey factual information. So long as it is assumed that the Bible is a collection of such statements, and that its entire function is to convey information or teaching that comes from God, then it might well make sense to ask of every statement whether it is true or false or to affirm that the Bible is entirely true. But this assumption needs careful examination. The Bible contains far more than factual statements, and we must examine in some detail the concept of 'truth'.

1. First, the Bible uses language in a great variety of ways, as has been excellently illustrated by G. B. Caird, *The Language and Imagery of the Bible* (London, 1980). Simple examples will make the point. In John 11:18 we have the comment 'Bethany is about fifteen stadia from Jerusalem'. That is a statement of fact which may or may not be true, and which can be verified or disproved. But in the same chapter we also have the command by Jesus, 'Take away the stone' (v. 39). It is nonsensical to ask whether this command is true or false because commands cannot be true or false. Similarly, when Jesus asks, 'Where have you laid him?' (v. 34), it is nonsensical to ask whether the question is true or false. Only statements can be true or false, not commands or questions. What does make sense is to ask whether the whole sentence, 'Jesus said, "Take away the stone"', which is a statement of fact, is true or false: did Jesus give such a command on the occasion specified, and were those his actual words?

Consequently, when I read in the declaration of faith of a Christian group the confession that everything that Jesus uttered is true, I must say that, literally understood, this is a meaningless confession unless the phrase 'everything that Jesus uttered' is restricted to mean 'every statement of fact uttered by Jesus'. In short, simply because of the nature of language, the terms 'true' and 'false' are not applicable to every individual statement in the Bible. The point may seem trivial to some readers, but it clearly shows at a very elementary level that to talk of the 'truth' of the Bible is to embark on a highly complex subject.

2. Then there is the fact that the question of truth may be answered in different ways at different levels of understanding. It is generally agreed that when Jesus told the story which begins, 'A certain man had two sons . . .', he was probably telling an invented story. If the question is asked, 'Is the story true?' the answer probably has to be 'No, it didn't happen like that'. But in fact the story is a parable, and the appropriate question to ask about a parable is not whether the events described actually happened, but whether the point made by the story is 'true' in the sense of being valid: is it true that God will treat us in the way that the father in the story treated his sons?

This is so obvious and so generally accepted that there is no need to labour it. But it does need to be extended. If it is recognised that the Bible contains parables which do not need to be literally and historically 'true' in order to be 'true' on the level of the message which they teach, then the same may be also the case with other non-factual ways of teaching. We find no difficulty with the use of metaphor and analogy and similar forms of language in this regard. When we read that a sharp two-edged sword proceeded from the mouth of the Lord (Rev. 1:16), we know not to take the description literally; it is true in another kind of way. Perhaps, then, we ought to find no difficulty with the use of myth and legend. There is no reason in principle why God should not be able to make use of such literary forms.

Why, then, is there such widespread feeling against them? The answer lies in the fact that some scholars persist in labelling as myth or legend passages which other scholars rightly or wrongly regard as historical. If there is good reason to believe that the story of Paul's conversion was intended to be genuine history, then to label it as 'legend' is unacceptable, especially if this label conveys the value judgment that it is false and worthless. If, however, a biblical writer was deliberately making use of myth or legend and was not aiming to write literal history, then we would be doing him a grave injustice and seriously mistreating the Scriptures if we were to insist that what was intended as myth or legend must be taken as fact. It is this kind of misunderstanding which has led to so much misinterpretation of the book of Revelation: what was meant from the beginning to be treated as symbolical, visionary language has been misunderstood as a literal chronological forecast of future events.

3. An understanding of the Bible as 'truth from God' may also lead to a failure to appreciate passages where God is not speaking to man. There are records of man speaking to God. He may be posing his questions to God, or he may be puzzling over them in his own mind, as in the case of Job, or he may be expressing his praise, thanks and petitions to God. Much of the book of Psalms is human response to God, human response that may have been providentially recorded as a pattern for us to imitate, but human response nevertheless. There are even passages which contain the words of the wicked and ignorant: what is a preacher to do with the utterances of Job's friends who are expressly said by God not to have spoken what is right concerning him (Job 42:7)? Are the closing words of Psalm 137 meant to give a form of human response in a tough situation that we ought to copy, or are they merely an accurate report of the wrong response of some Jews to their captors?

It can of course be argued that the 'truth' of the Bible in such instances lies in the fact that what these various people said is accurately reported. But this is 'truth' at a comparatively superficial level, and the real question is what kind of truth, if any, we are to attribute to the significance of what is said. The point is surely that there is a certain widening of horizons here. The Bible functions not just as a record of God's teaching to man, but also as a record of how people have thought about God and responded to him. When people do have wrong thoughts about God, one hopes that it is not being suggested that God inspired them to do so. The Bible gives us, we must say, not simply a recital of historical events which functioned as divine revelation, but rather an account of historical events in the midst of which a revelation of God took place. So from this point of view what is at issue is not so much the truth of the Bible as a source of divine revelation but rather the truth of the Bible in its depiction of the human situation in which God revealed himself.

4. A further question about biblical truth may be – 'true for whom?' In Leviticus and Deuteronomy we find legislation regarding the distinction between clean and unclean foods which was binding on the Israelites at the time when it was promulgated. But God himself declared that these laws were no longer valid, whether for Jews or Gentiles, in Acts 10:15, and Mark recognised that the teaching of Jesus was to the same effect (Mark 7:19). Thus in the light of New Testament teaching these laws no longer convey God's commands to the Christian and they are not 'true' in the sense of being valid for him; on the contrary, if anybody tried to insist on Christians keeping these rules, he would be disobeying God's commands to his people now. Perhaps one might look for a 'deeper sense' in the food laws and suggest, for example, that they testify to some basic kind of distinction which must still be observed. But if we do this, we are implicitly recognising that the laws can no longer be interpreted in the way in which their original readers were meant to take them.

The same thing could be said of the laws about sacrificial ritual. They were valid for their own time, and they may be interpreted as 'types' pointing forward to the one, true sacrifice of Jesus, but in the eyes of the writer to the Hebrews it would be positively sinful for Christians to keep them literally.

It follows that some passages of Scripture which once were true in the sense of containing God's binding commands are no longer true in the sense of being binding upon us. The passages may be true as records of what God said in the past; they are not true in the sense that they still convey his will to us today.

We can sum up this part of our discussion by saying that the concept of 'truth' is a complex one, and that it is not easy to apply it to every part of the Bible. From the point of view of

Christian practice today it is indeed somewhat banal to be told that Leviticus 11 is a true record of what God said to the Israelites if it is no longer relevant for us in any real sense of the term. What our discussion has brought out is something of the broader character of the Bible; it is not simply a record of divine revelation to mankind, but it also contains a record of the historical setting in which revelation came (and without which it cannot be fully understood), and it presents a progressive revelation, parts of which are now superseded in the light of what followed.

Nevertheless, we must go on to ask whether the Bible really is 'true' in the areas where it may be tested. Or, to put the point otherwise, in what ways does the Bible need to be true in order to fulfil its God-intended purpose, and is it in fact true in these ways? These questions are difficult to formulate clearly, and difficult to answer satisfactorily. We have to admit that trying to 'test' the Bible to see whether it conveys truth is possible only in limited areas. Broadly speaking, we can draw a distinction between statements which may be capable of testing and those which cannot be tested. The distinction is roughly that between historical statements and theological statements. For example, it is in principle open to historical study whether or not Paul journeyed to Damascus at a particular time and experienced a shattering vision on the way. However, it is not possible to prove by historical methods whether or not this vision was in fact what he says it was, namely a real appearance of the risen Lord Jesus. Regarding the historical question of whether Paul had a shattering experience, it may not be possible to prove conclusively that it did or did not happen; we are dependent on the reports in Acts and the hints in Paul's letters, which there is good reason to accept as trustworthy, but the matter cannot be proved or disproved beyond all doubt. Even, therefore, on the historical level there is often no sure proof one way or the other. Regarding the theological question, even if the historical fact of the vision is proved beyond doubt, we have no way of proving that it actually was the risen Jesus who appeared to Paul; that is a theological statement which cannot be proved or disproved. How would one prove to a sceptic that Paul had not suffered from an hallucination? Of course, one can appeal to the reality of Christian experience, but this is simply to underline the fact that the question is again one of faith.

If it could be proved historically that Paul never made the journey in question and never saw a vision of any kind, then the theological question would automatically be answered in the negative: Paul did not see the risen Lord. This is why the historical questions cannot be evaded: the historical and the theological statements in the Bible are closely interrelated. It is, therefore, very understandable that part of a belief in the entire trustworthiness of the Bible as the revelation of God's way of salvation is that it should be trustworthy on a historical level.

If the debate is conducted in terms of inerrancy, the problem is usually dealt with by claiming that, even if the Bible contains what appear to be historical errors, contradictions and so on, either these are not 'really' errors when assessed by the appropriate standards or there must be some explanation of them which will preserve the accuracy of the Biblical record, even if it cannot at present be provided. The Chicago Statement states this position:

> We affirm that canonical Scripture should always be interpreted on the basis that it is infallible and inerrant. . . . Apparent inconsistencies should not be ignored. Solution of them, where this can be convincingly achieved, will encourage our faith, and where for the present no convincing solution is at hand we shall significantly honor God by trusting His assurance that His Word is true, despite these appearances, and by maintaining our confidence that one day they will be seen to have been illusions.

This is a classical Christian position which can be traced back at least as far as Augustine. It is open to the objection that, if this view is accepted, then no evidence to the contrary is ever admissible, since it can always be urged that a solution to every difficulty will be found some day. We shall return to this point later, but for the moment we may comment that it is not as odd a position as it may seem to be to its opponents and critics. In principle it is not dissimilar from that of the Christian who holds on to his faith in God despite every apparent piece of evidence to the contrary and refuses to capitulate to unbelief. Nevertheless, there is something strange about beliefs which are totally invulnerable, and defenders of this view perhaps need to face up to the question: what combination of circumstances would constitute a refutation of my belief?

An important practical point also arises. How is it to be decided what kind of phenomena in the Bible are not to be classed as 'real errors', and what kind of phenomena are to be regarded as 'real errors' which need some explanation not at present available or else must be regarded as calling the theory of inerrancy in question? Or, to put the problem in our own terms, what sort of statements in the Bible would be incompatible with a belief in its entire trustworthiness for its divinely intended purpose?

The Chicago Statement is well aware of the problem:

> The truthfulness of Scripture is not negated by the appearance in it of irregularities of grammar or spelling, phenomenal descriptions of nature, reports of false statements (e.g. the lies of Satan), or seeming discrepancies between one passage and another.

And again:

> When total precision of a particular kind was not expected nor aimed at, it is no error not to have achieved it. Scripture is inerrant, not in the sense of being absolutely precise by modern standards, but in the sense of making good its claims and achieving that measure of focused truth at which its authors aimed.

Here it is being admitted that certain phenomena, which might well be regarded as errors and contradictions, must not be counted as such. The reason for making this concession is that no amount of exegetical ingenuity can avoid recognising the presence of such phenomena in the Bible. The significant point is that, once this has been admitted, then it has been implicitly agreed that the definition of the kind of truth to be found in the Bible is dependent upon biblical interpretation of the difficult passages and cannot be drawn simply from statements in the Bible about its own nature. In other words, the principle that 'Scripture should always be interpreted on the basis that it is infallible and inerrant' still leaves open the question of the kind of infallibility and inerrancy to be ascribed to the Bible, and this can be determined only by an examination of what actually happens in the Bible. We must now look at some of the problems that arise. For we certainly cannot be satisfied with a statement which cheerfully declares that 'the truthfulness of Scripture is not negated by . . . seeming discrepancies between one passage and another': major discrepancies cannot be ignored in this way.

There is the problem of historical approximation. In the story of Jairus as recorded by Matthew it is simply said that when Jairus first met Jesus he told him that his daughter was dead (Matt. 9:18). According to Mark and Luke, however, the daughter was merely on the point of death at the beginning of the story and it was only later – after the incident of the woman with the haemorrhage – that Jairus and Jesus learned that she had actually died (Mark 5:35 f.; Luke 8:49 f.). There is a clear contradiction between the initial words of Jairus as recorded by Matthew and the other Evangelists. We can, of course, explain the contradiction quite easily and acceptably by saying that Matthew, whose general policy was to tell stories about Jesus in fewer words than Mark, has abbreviated the story and given the general sense of what happened without going into details. But the fact still remains that Matthew has attributed to Jairus words which he did not actually say at the time stated.

Other examples of imprecision can be easily produced. The sayings of Jesus were probably mostly uttered in Aramaic, the Jewish vernacular of the time. Our Gospels written in Greek give us translations of them and not the actual words which he spoke. In a number of cases (especially where we can compare varying versions of the same sayings in different Gospels) we have the general sense rather than the actual words. We may compare 'Behold, those who wear soft raiment are in kings' houses' (Matt. 11:8) with 'Behold, those who are gorgeously apparelled and live in luxury are in kings' courts' (Luke 7:25). The Bible does not give us absolute historical precision, and indeed it does not claim to do so. We do not need absolute precision in such matters as these, where God has evidently chosen not to give us it.

A second problem is the presence of interpretation. Any historical report inevitably reflects the stance of the reporter, and any historical event is so complex that it can be reported only from a particular angle and in a selective manner. A stock example is the story of King Omri. The account of his reign in 1 Kings 16:15–28 mentions how he came to the throne, how he made Samaria his capital city, and how he did evil in the sight of the Lord by worshipping idols. There is not a word of the fact, attested by secular sources of the period, that he had a reputation as one of the most powerful Israelite kings, responsible for the conquest of Moab, and so outstanding indeed that for the next one hundred and fifty years Assyrian sources called Israel 'the land of Omri'. If the picture of Omri in the Old Testament is not distorted, it is at least very one-sided.

Or one might observe the way in which the impression given in the Gospels of the Pharisees in the time of Jesus is almost uniformly bad. The sharp words of criticism which Jesus justifiably uttered against the formality and hypocrisy of their legalistic religion have been preserved, as have the accounts of incidents which indicate the suspicion and hostility of the Pharisees towards Jesus. Yet we find that Paul did not wholly repudiate his upbringing as a Pharisee, and could claim that it was as an upholder of the Pharisaic point of view over against that of the Sadducees that he was accused by the Sanhedrin (Acts 23:6). Not all Pharisees were hypocrites, and not all of Pharisaic teaching was legalistic and unhelpful.

Again it is clear that for good reasons the Evangelists have presented one side of the picture. From a historical point of view we have not been given the whole truth; God's purpose in the composition of Scripture did not require that we should have both sides of the picture.

A third problem is that of possible historical error. In Acts 5:33–39 a speech attributed to Gamaliel refers to risings made by Theudas and Judas the Galilean. The problems are that a rising by a man called Theudas is said by Josephus, the Jewish historian of the time, to have taken place after the rising of Judas and not before it (contrary to the order in Acts 5:37), and after the date at which Gamaliel must have made his speech. (According to Josephus, *Antiquities* 20:97 f., Judas rose in A.D. 6, and Theudas during the governorship of Fadus (A.D. 44–46); Gamaliel's speech must have taken place soon after A.D. 30.) Many scholars would say that Luke has committed an anachronism. But it could be said that, even if this is the case, the force of the illustrations is unaffected. Theudas did attempt a rebellion and he did come to naught, whatever be the date of the incident. The illustration proves its point for Luke's readers. Indeed, the same point might have been made by a fictitious story, although I would strongly argue that the point depends on showing that this kind of thing actually happens in history and not just in fiction.

But, granted that the point is valid for Luke's readers independent of the date of the incident, we still face the fact of an apparent historical error by Luke. How do we respond to it?

It may be possible to produce a convincing explanation of the text which will preserve Luke's accuracy. It could be argued that Josephus got his dates wrong (the view taken by the Jerusalem Bible). This, however, is very unlikely. A better solution would be that Luke was referring to a different, earlier Theudas who is otherwise unknown. But this is pure hypothesis; the likelihood of two rebels with the same rather unusual name is low, and is not on a par with the fact that Josephus knew of four men called Simon and three called Judas, all of whom led rebellions in a period of half a century. This solution, therefore, is not very probable.

Alternatively, it may be claimed that there is no need to produce a convincing solution, but only to show that a solution is possible. Coincidences do happen, and there could have been an earlier Theudas. Perhaps evidence will yet turn up to show that there was.

The defender of inerrancy has to adopt this kind of approach whenever he is faced with an insoluble difficulty of this kind. He has an invulnerable position, since he holds that in principle there can be no 'real' errors in the Bible, and he is prepared to argue that any hypothetical solution to an alleged difficulty, no matter how improbable it may seem to ordinary historical judgment, is always more probable than the hypothesis that the Bible may be in error.

There are certainly occasions when this kind of argument is legitimate, and it is not peculiar to defenders of biblical inerrancy. If a scientist adopts a hypothesis which he finds generally convincing, he will continue to maintain it despite evidence to the contrary and attempt to find some way of explaining that evidence. If, however, the evidence proves intractable, he will attempt to reformulate his hypothesis accordingly – and this is where he differs from the strict inerrantist. In this particular instance it can certainly be argued that Luke's historical accuracy in other cases where it can be tested is a strong argument in favour of giving him the benefit of the doubt with regard to Theudas. It may not be so easy to argue the same point for other biblical writers whose historical accuracy is suspect.

But the flaw in the argument for inerrancy here is that a particular view of the nature of Scripture is being assumed. What we are trying to do is to find out from the Bible itself what its character is, and what is involved in inerrancy. Defenders of inerrancy have already had to admit that Scripture is not 'absolutely precise by modern standards'; we are trying to define the meaning of that phrase by looking at Scripture itself.

This brings us to the third possible response. It can be argued that here we have a genuine historical mistake, and that the presence of this and other mistakes demonstrates that our understanding of the truth of the Bible must allow for such things. Many readers may contemplate this possibility with horror and be tempted to read no further, while to others it may seem to be only good sense.

It is arguable that the theory of strict factual inerrancy is like the theory that the sun and the other planets revolve round the earth. My understanding is that so many complications had to be introduced to make this simple theory fit in with the facts revealed by increasingly detailed and accurate astronomical observations that eventually, although the geocentric theory remained mathematically possible (but inordinately complex), it was more sensible to abandon it and adopt the view that all the planets revolve round the sun – and this in the end proved to be a more fruitful hypothesis. Now when we bear in mind that the theory of biblical inerrancy collapses totally if *only one* factual error is proved to exist, and when we further remember that many people find almost innumerable possibilities of factual error in the Bible, it is not surprising that they conclude that the theory of inerrancy involves too many unlikelihoods, and that therefore the probabilities are against it. Even if a solution could be found to the problem in Acts 5, some other problem could instantly be produced to take its place.

It may be, therefore, that the evidence requires us to accept the presence of historical mistakes in the Bible, and we then have to ask whether this is compatible with a belief in its entire trustworthiness for its divinely intended purpose. Obviously, this possibility could not be confined to the purely 'historical' parts of the Bible; as we have seen, it is impossible to draw an arbitrary line between the historical and the theological and thus to claim that the latter area is exempt. Some scholars have experimented with such a concept of 'partial infallibility', but it is simply not viable; historical reporting is inevitably bound up with theological interpretation, and no hard and fast line can be drawn between history and theology.

Our discussion suggests that there are three positions that may be held. First, there is the 'inerrantist' views, which claims that there cannot be historical, scientific and theological errors in the Bible, although it does allow for some degree of imprecision. Second, there is the concept of 'infallibility' or 'entire trustworthiness' which allows that a greater amount of imprecision than a strict inerrantist might admit is not only present in the Bible but is also quite compatible with its divine purpose. Third, there is the 'liberal' type of view which finds a much higher degree of imprecision, amounting to much error, in the Bible and holds that any suggestion of infallibility or inerrancy is to be rejected. There is a vast difference between the second and third of these views, between allowing that the Bible may contain a certain amount of imprecision and asserting that it is riddled with errors and contradictions. But there is much less difference between the first and second views; what the second view is saying, in effect, is that a greater amount of latitude is needed in determining what level of 'precision' God regarded as compatible with the trustworthy communication of his self-revelation in Scripture. To put the point another way, if a defender of the first view accuses an upholder of the second view of allowing the presence of errors in Scripture, the latter can reply: 'Judged by the appropriate standards what you regard as "errors" are not to be regarded as such when assessed in terms of God's purpose'. Both views deny that the Bible contains statements which are incompatible with its character as the Word of God.

Thus the distinction between the first and second views is very much a matter of definition. The gulf between them and the third view is much wider, involving the problem of whether the Bible contains such erroneous statements that it must be regarded as a fallible, human document through which nevertheless God can speak to us. This raises the whole question of biblical criticism which we shall discuss in the next chapter. Meanwhile, we must take up another area of discussion which may throw some light on the difference between the first and second views. We can place our discussion in a broader perspective by considering the character of the Bible as we actually have it and use it today. There are three aspects to this problem.

First, the actual wording of the text of the Bible is not

certain. Nearly every English translation of the Bible has a number of footnotes which indicate places where the various manuscripts have preserved different forms of wording in a given verse, and where scientific study of the text is not able to affirm with absolute certainty which form of words is the original. Nobody can be sure, for example, whether John described Jesus in John 1:18 as 'the only Son' or 'the only God'. It is true that the number of such places in the New Testament is limited, and often the uncertainties do not greatly affect our understanding of the text. There are similar problems in the Old Testament, including places where the wording seems to have been corrupted in the course of transmission and nobody knows for certain how to restore the correct wording.

Now it can be argued that the textual problems are often concerned with insignificant variations in wording, and that in any case inerrancy is to be credited only to the actual writings of the original authors and not to subsequent copies. This does not affect the basic fact that we do not know for certain exactly what the original wording was; all that we can be sure of is that no existing version of the Bible, in its original languages or in translation, is free from error in reproducing the original wording. God has not thought it necessary that we should have an error-free version of the text. And there do exist examples where the uncertainty affects important theological points. It is obviously a matter of great significance whether Luke 23:34 is part of the Gospel or not. And yet we have to live with such uncertainties.

Second, there are problems about the interpretation of the Bible. This is demonstrated by the differences in wording between the various translations of the Bible and by the vast number of commentaries that continue to be written. Translations represent the interpretations of the text held by translators. For example, the Greek word translated 'only' in John 1:18 can also be translated as 'only begotten'; the *New International Version* in its standard edition adopts the former word, but the Gideons organisation felt so strongly that the latter translation was correct that they had an alteration made in the edition prepared for distribution by them. Here we have a place where the meaning is ambiguous, and where competent scholars agree to differ.

Not only are there ambiguous statements, there are also places where the meaning is so obscure that nobody knows for certain what was in the original author's mind. What, for example, did Matthew think that Jesus meant when he said, 'Truly I say to you, you will not have gone through all the towns of Israel, before the Son of man comes' (Matt. 10:23)? Or what did Paul mean when he wrote that the law was 'ordained by angels through an intermediary. Now an intermediary implies more than one; but God is one' (Gal. 3:19 f.)? Many suggestions have been offered, but nobody really knows what was meant.

God has not given us a Bible which is perfectly clear to understand. Certainly, the main lines of interpretation are clear, and we can rightly speak of the perspicuity of the Bible. But there are enough uncertainties and obscurities to have kept an army of commentators busy right from the earliest days of the Church. Whether or not the original text is free from error, we are not free from error and uncertainty in understanding it. And yet we have to live with this situation.

Third, when we come to the area of application of what the Bible teaches, we land in further uncertainties. There is a cleavage among Bible-believing Christians between those who hold that baptism should be administered to believers who are old enough to know what they are doing, and those who hold that baptism should be administered to the infant children of believers. Both groups claim to be bound by the teaching of the Bible, but they differ over how that teaching is to be applied in the Church today. We might well wish that God had given us such clear teaching that all Christians would agree on this and other matters, but the fact is that he has not done so. Both sides have to admit that they and those who differ from them are conscientiously trying to follow out biblical teaching. And yet we have to live with this situation.

Sufficient has been said to make our point. Whether or not the Bible, as originally written, is free from error, the subsequent transmission and understanding of it is not free from error. No translation is absolutely accurate, and no commentary gets every detail of the meaning correct. Consequently the question arises: if God's purpose in giving us a Bible which is entirely trustworthy for his purposes did not include the provision of a guaranteed text, a guaranteed interpretation and a guaranteed application for today, what right have we to assume that he gave an original text that was guaranteed to be utterly precise? The inerrantist will reply that, even if we may make errors in understanding, at least we can have an objective, reliable basis from which to start, and the fact of uncertainties in later transmission is not incompatible with this. This may be logically correct, but it can be argued that the fact that entire trustworthiness is compatible with textual uncertainties and problems in interpretation suggests that it is also compatible with a certain lack of precision in the original text. In short, with so much uncertainty at the level of interpretation, a further measure of uncertainty at the level of the original text does not greatly affect the situation, and is in line with the character of God's providential care for the transmission of the Bible.

It is time to summarise. We started from the view that the Bible is entirely trustworthy for the purposes for which God has inspired it. This appears to be a reasonable deduction from the biblical doctrine of inspiration, free from the difficulties which surround the attempt to derive inerrancy from inspiration. We have seen, however, that the Bible has not been handed down in the form of a perfectly accurate text which can be interpreted throughout without the possibility of error. Further, we found that the Bible does not function solely as a means of conveying revelatory information from God, and that the concept of its truthfulness is highly complex. Against this background we have asked whether the Bible contains errors and contradictions. It certainly does contain statements which can be regarded as erroneous by some standards but which are consistent with its intended purpose; one does not fault a carpenter for measuring a table leg accurately to only one decimal place when the standard of accuracy in a laboratory runs to several places of decimals. The problem, then, is what degree of imprecision is compatible with the intended purpose of the Bible.

Here we have encountered two points of view. One group of scholars defends inerrancy. They argue that inspiration implies inerrancy, and that the inerrancy of the Bible is a fact which can be defended. All cases of alleged error can be either accommodated within the definition of inerrancy or assumed to be merely apparent errors. The other group of scholars defends the entire trustworthiness of the Bible for the purpose for which God inspired it; inspiration means that God made the Bible what he wanted it to be for his purposes. This school of thought holds that a greater degree of imprecision may be compatible with God's purposes. It will be apparent that the former group holds that the Bible was the result of a process giving the same results as divine dictation, while the latter group leaves the precise mode of inspiration somewhat uncertain.

I have tried to present these two points of view fairly, and if the discussion has tended to emphasise the second point of view, it is because it is not so well known and is a possible option. But at the end of the day the difference between the two points of view may well be nothing more than one of degree. I have already quoted from the Chicago Statement regarding the kind of phenomena which are said to be compatible with biblical inerrancy. Let me further quote a related passage:

We deny that it is proper to evaluate Scripture according to standards of truth and error that are alien to its usage or purpose. We further deny that inerrancy is negated by biblical phenomena such as a lack of modern technical precision, irregularities of grammar or spelling, observational descriptions of nature, the reporting of falsehood, the use of hyperbole and round numbers, the topical arrangement of material, variant selections of material in parallel accounts, or the use of free citations.

70

It is clear that it is a matter of biblical interpretation to decide what is or is not compatible with biblical inerrancy. If we are to evaluate Scripture according to its own standards of truth and error, then it is arguable that the Bible does contain what may be regarded as errors and contradictions by modern standards but which are not in fact contrary to its own standards and purpose. If the inerrantists are standing for the truth of Scripture, understood in scriptural terms, then their position is no different in principle from that of the other school of evangelical Christians who also affirm the entire trustworthiness of Scripture. There may be differences between the two schools on matters of detail which are in danger of being elevated into matters of principle, but these are as nothing compared with that which they have in common, namely the belief in the entire trustworthiness of Scripture for its God-given purpose. And there is a world of difference between this position and that which would deny that the Scriptures are the inspired Word of God.

Nevertheless, there are upholders of biblical inerrancy who would argue that, even though evangelical Christians who hold a different view of Scripture from them insist that it is simply a matter of degree, in fact their position is the beginning of a slippery slope which leads away from other fundamental doctrines in the long run. It is an example of the so-called 'domino' theory, which says that if you knock over one of a series of contiguous dominoes standing on their ends, then the effect will spread to all the other dominoes and in the end none will be left standing.

It is a problem how seriously this objection is to be taken. It is, of course, an analogy, and as such has no power to prove anything, unless it can be shown that the things being compared are closely similar. If one were to push the analogy, one might suggest that it implies that the doctrine of Scripture, especially of inerrancy, is no more firmly grounded than a domino standing in rather a wobbly manner on its end. The truth of the matter is that Christian doctrines are interrelated, and a person who does not accept the supreme authority of Scripture is not likely to feel bound by its doctrinal teaching in detail. If, however, doctrines are inter-related, then the better analogy may be not a set of separate dominoes weakly balanced against one another but rather a set of links in a piece of chain-mail, each securely fastened to its neighbours and strengthening the whole.

The question then becomes whether a specific understanding of the nature of the Bible in terms of inerrancy is essential if the doctrine of Scripture is to play its part in the whole web of Christian teaching. Obviously the doctrine of Scripture is more than a mere link in the system, but occupies a fundamental position as the basis of other teachings. Three things can be said. First, acceptance of biblical inerrancy is no guarantee of the doctrinal orthodoxy upheld by evangelical Christianity; there have been plenty of odd positions upheld by defenders of inerrancy. Second, the entire trustworthiness of Scripture for its divinely intended purposes is an adequate formula to cover the need for a secure basis for doctrine. Third, we have in the end to be content with what God has actually given us and not with what we may wish that he had given us. It may be objected that to put the matter this way is to make the teaching of Scripture a relative rather than an absolute standard. This is simply not so. The authority of Scripture remains absolute. Any element of relativism comes in at the stage of interpreting what Scripture says, since its meaning is not always crystal clear, and here the inerrantist is as much in difficulty as anybody else, since (as we have seen) he still has to interpret Scripture to find out what its inerrant message is.

Perhaps one may say that the problem is one of definition and where to draw the line. It is worth asking whether 'inerrant' is really the most appropriate word to use to describe Scripture. It needs so much qualification, even by its defenders, that it is in danger of dying the death of a thousand qualifications. The term 'infallible' in the sense of 'entirely trustworthy' is undoubtedly preferable. Certainly, if I were to be put in a corner and had only the two options open to me of confessing the Bible to be inerrant or errant, then I have no doubt in which direction I would cast my vote as most nearly expressing my understanding of the nature of the Bible; I would prefer, however, to frame the options differently.

Belief in 'the divine inspiration and infallibility of Holy Scripture' may be in the end a matter of faith, but it is a most reasonable faith. Or is it? We have still to face up to the questions raised by biblical criticism, a form of study which has often led people to see the Bible as a highly fallible set of documents. Can we really maintain the entire trustworthiness of the Bible in the teeth of biblical criticism? Some conservative writers would rule biblical criticism out of court because of the sceptical conclusions to which it often comes: are they right to do so, or are they being obscurantist in their attitude? These are the questions to which we must next turn.

4

HOW ARE WE TO STUDY THE BIBLE?

It is scarcely an exaggeration to say that the questions which
concern us in this book are all questions about how the Bible
is to be interpreted. To answer the question 'What does the
Bible say about itself?' is to gather together various biblical
statements and to try to understand what they say and how
they are to be related to one another. To frame a doctrine of
inspiration is to take the process of interpretation a step
further by looking for a hypothesis which will explain what the
biblical writers say about their work. And in our discussion
of the results of inspiration it became evident that the
question of the infallibility of the Bible is very much a
question of interpretation in that we had to decide what
phenomena in the Bible might be held to militate against a
belief in its infallibility.

Despite this fairly clear evidence that the Bible needs to be
interpreted, there are still people who think that the Bible
does not need interpretation, or at least that it requires very
little. Its message is held to be so clear that there is no need for
complicated biblical scholarship. It is enough to read the
Bible and let God speak through its pages. Has it not been
said that we are to interpret Scripture in the light of Scripture?
Recently I heard of a Bible College where the students were
encouraged to begin by studying the Bible without any scholarly aids whatever in order that they might understand it on
its own terms, free from all presuppositions.

Other people have been brought up to study the Bible 'like
any other book' (to use the famous phrase of B. Jowett), and
they feel that they must go into all the problems raised by
biblical criticism, such as the J, E, D and P theory of the
composition of the first five books of the Old Testament,

75

before they can begin to understand and apply it. Such study soon leads to the discovery of problems; in fact even without such study people may quickly come up against worrying problems. A recent book by David Winter, *But This I Can Believe* (London, 1980), has outlined some of the problems that people find when they read the Bible critically. Did the Christmas story really happen precisely as it is told? Precisely as it is told, however, in which Gospel (for some would argue that the stories in Matthew and Luke are not completely harmonisable)? Have we to believe in all the miracles? And so on.

Here are two very different approaches. The former can lead to a total anti-intellectualism which is blind to its own presuppositions and so misinterprets the Bible, and which simply ignores the very real problems which the Bible presents. The latter can lead to people getting so hung up on the problems that they never come within reach of hearing and obeying the message of the Bible. These are, no doubt, extreme possibilities, but they represent real tendencies. The unfortunate thing is the hostility that has developed between the two broad groupings.

It is easy to see how this has arisen. After centuries of biblical study which had largely failed to recognise the problems raised by the biblical text, the eighteenth and nineteenth centuries saw the development of 'higher criticism'. It was so named because it came as the second step after 'lower criticism'. The latter is the attempt to determine the original wording of the Bible by means of textual study of the manuscripts. Higher criticism, building on this foundation, deals with the authorship, situation and sources of the various books of the Bible. The study often reached conclusions that appeared to be incompatible with a belief in the inspiration of the Bible. The discovery of sources behind the so-called 'books of Moses' and the suggestion that these books were written for the most part at a period later than that of Moses were felt to be contrary to the theory of biblical inspiration. Often the existence of sources was detected by drawing attention to contradictions between different parts of a story.

The historicity of miraculous events was questioned by scholars who seemed to have a bias against the supernatural and even to act on the presupposition that such events were in principle impossible. Critics appeared to pick and choose which parts of the Bible they were prepared to believe according to their own whim. It is no wonder that many Christians felt inclined to wash their hands of the whole approach, and this attitude still persists. Surely, they argue, the method is riddled to the core with unbelief, it is of no profit to the reader of the Bible, and it should be set aside. It is equally unsurprising that this attitude in its turn should be rejected and scorned by the defenders of a scholarly approach to the Bible, arguing that we must follow the evidence where it leads us and not rule out critical study on principle.

How, then, are we to study the Bible? The question is a large one, and we shall divide our treatment between this and the next chapter, considering first the more technical aspects of biblical criticism and then the problems that arise in finding the significance of the Bible for today.

An extended example may help to focus our discussion. In the Authorised Version we find the verse: 'If any man loveth not the Lord, let him be anathema. Maran atha.' (1 Cor. 16:22). We would not even be able to read this verse if it had not already been studied in Greek and translated into English for our benefit by scholars. That single point should be enough in itself to demonstrate to us that biblical *study* using other books alongside the Bible as aids (Greek dictionaries, grammars, and so on) is absolutely indispensable; if we do not do the task ourselves, somebody else must do it on our behalf.

Even as the verse stands in translation, it still contains two difficult words. One of them, *anathema*, may be intelligible enough. It is actually a Greek word which has been taken over directly into English; it means 'an accursed thing' and came to mean 'excommunicated'. The other word, *Maran atha*, is probably less intelligible despite its appearance in an English version of the Bible. The only place one is likely to find it outside the Bible and books about it is as a name for a Christian holiday home or conference centre. We can understand its meaning only thanks to a knowledge (whether our own or somebody else's) of the language to which it belongs, and which, as it happens, is neither Greek nor Hebrew, but Aramaic. Even a knowledge of Aramaic will not immediately solve the question since, owing to the ambiguities of that language, the phrase can be translated as 'Our Lord, come!' or 'Our Lord has come' or 'Our Lord will come'.

But what is the 'coming' which is in mind? Basically there are two possibilities. One is that the phrase is a prayer to the Lord to come *in the future* as our judge and saviour, or else it is a declaration of confidence that he will do so. The other possibility is that it is a prayer for his presence *here and now*, probably at the Lord's Supper, or else it is a declaration of confidence that he is already present. Further study is needed to decide which of these two possibilities is the more likely. Since Paul looks forward to the future coming of the Lord earlier in the same letter (1 Cor. 11:26 – in the context of the Lord's Supper), and since the same expectation is expressed in the same words (but in Greek) in Revelation 22:20 (see also Phil. 4:5), I prefer the former of the two possibilities. Here is a statement of early Christian belief and hope.

Before going any further, we may pause to observe that we have now shown that all of us do practise biblical criticism to some extent. 'Criticism' in this case simply means 'study', and we cannot avoid practising it if we want to find out what any text in the New Testament is saying. Either we do it ourselves, or we get somebody else to do it for us (a Bible translator or commentator), but apart from it the Bible is largely a closed book and 'Maran atha' is simply a vague, pious-sounding name for a Christian guest house. To understand this one phrase we need a knowledge of the Aramaic language, the ability to relate this text to other relevant passages in the New Testament, and a general knowledge of the history and practice of the early Church; we also need (this is the theme of the next chapter) some general principles for deciding how we apply biblical teaching to the life of the Church today.

But we have not yet reached the end of the problems raised by this text. One particular aspect of it invites and positively compels us to go further. This is the odd fact that Paul suddenly breaks out into Aramaic in a letter written in Greek. Why does he do so? There is a comparable case in Romans 8:15 where he uses the Aramaic word *abba* which means 'father'. Here he is quoting a word used by Jesus (Mark 14:36), and he quotes it in Aramaic because that was the language in which it was first used – just as we may say 'Amen' or 'Hallelujah'. So here too he uses an Aramaic word because he is quoting a statement or prayer used by early Christians who spoke that language. This leads us back to investigate the origin of this phrase.

Two different theories have been suggested in answer to this problem. A German scholar, W. Bousset, held that the phrase arose in the Christian church at Antioch, whose members spoke both Aramaic and Greek. He held that the title of 'Lord' was used for the gods worshipped by pagans in their religious cults (as 1 Cor. 8:5 indicates), and that Christians took over the title and applied it to Jesus. Thus originally the effect of giving this title to Jesus was to understand him in the same kind of way as a pagan deity. Moreover, Bousset argued that this was an innovation in Christian belief as the Church moved out into the pagan world, and he was quite emphatic that the earliest members of the Church did not view Jesus in this way; for them he was simply the Messiah and the Son of man. A high reverence for Jesus as Lord developed only gradually in the Church in its pagan environment, and one gains the impression that for Bousset it was not necessarily a desirable development.

But there is a second theory about our text. M. Black noted that it bears a close similarity to some words from the Jewish book of 1 Enoch which are quoted in Jude 14: 'Behold, the Lord came with his holy myriads to execute judgment on all'. It so happens that some parts of the book of Enoch have survived in Aramaic in the caves at Qumran near the Dead Sea. This discovery shows that this Jewish book existed in Aramaic at the time of the early Church. Black has pointed out that if we translate the Greek text of 1 Enoch back into Aramaic we obtain the same phrase as Paul uses in 1

Corinthians; unfortunately not enough of the Aranauc text of 1 Enoch has survived to confirm this suggestion, but it is an eminently reasonable one. From this observation follows the probability that the Aramaic phrase used by Paul was taken from 1 Enoch with one important change: what was said about *God* coming in the future to exercise judgment was applied to *Jesus* by the use of the word 'Lord', which for a Jew signified God but for a Christian signified Jesus. If this view is correct, then the Christian use of the words probably arose in Palestine among Aramaic-speaking members of the early Church.

What is the point of all this technical discussion? We have been trying to find out where Paul got this particular phrase *Maran atha* from, and how it was used before it reached him. This is surely a legitimate question to ask, just as when a New Testament writer prefaces a statement with the words 'as it is written' it is natural to discover where the quotation comes from.

If we make this enquiry, then we may well find that it sheds light on the use of the phrase by Paul and thus help us to understand better what he was saying. In the present case three points emerge. First, if the phrase *Maran atha* is ultimately based on 1 Enoch, this adds considerable weight to the argument that it refers to the future coming of the Lord in judgment rather than to his spiritual coming in the Lord's Supper. (It is, of course, possible that both comings are in mind, but, if so, it is the future coming which is of primary importance.) Second, again if the phrase comes from 1 Enoch, we have an important example of a text which originally applied to Yahweh, God the Father, and which was then reapplied to Jesus with the implication that he exercises the judgmental prerogative of God and so has a unique status alongside the Father. There are other places in the New Testament where Old Testament texts are used in the same way, but it is helpful to have yet another example of this phenomenon which demonstrates how highly Christians estimated Jesus. And, third, undoubtedly other objects of worship were called 'Lord' in the ancient world; by their adoption of this term, which originally referred to God the Father, Christians were declaring the superiority of Jesus over any other so-called lords:

> Jesus! the name high over all,
> In hell, or earth, or sky;
> Angels and men before it fall,
> And devils fear and fly.

All this is helpful insight that comes from probing into the origins of Paul's thinking, and justifies doing so. But some other points have arisen which may cause disquiet, and we mut now look at these.

To begin with, if the suggestion by Black is correct, then this Christian phrase was drawn from a Jewish book that was not part of the canon of the Old Testament. (Even, incidentally, if Black is wrong, it is still true that 1 Enoch is quoted in the New Testament by Jude.) If we follow the views of Bousset, then the application of the title 'Lord' to Jesus was derived from pagan religion. Probably nobody is worried by the fact that New Testament writers used the Old Testament as a theological quarry. But some people may have qualms about such a dubious book as 1 Enoch being used alongside the Old Testament as a source for ideas to be used in Christian theology, and they may be much more disturbed by the derivation of the title of 'Lord' from paganism.

However, this appeal to a non-Christian background seems to me to be fully justifiable. The citation of 1 Enoch does not mean that it was regarded as Christian Scripture, but that its words were found to be an apt statement of what Christians believed would happen in the future. Christians cannot have been unaware that the title of 'Lord' was used for pagan gods and also that it was applied to the emperor with the implication that he was supreme on earth and possibly also divine as well; the term certainly indicated divinity or was associated with divinity by the end of the first century A.D. Christians later refused to use the term with reference to the emperor because they held that Jesus alone was worthy of the title. In other words, they said, 'Whatever this title means when applied by pagans to their idols or to the emperor, for us it means these things only when applied to Jesus. He is supreme'. Thus to some extent the status of Jesus was defined by contrast with that of pagan gods and the emperor, and one might say that it was just this contrast which helped to sharpen the Christians' appreciation of what it meant to call Jesus 'Lord'. Thus there would seem to be no real problem about accepting that Christians were influenced by their Jewish and pagan environment. If this is a fresh idea to some readers, or one that they have not fully realised previously, then here is a case where biblical study opens up new ways of understanding.

However, it could be argued that our study has other, disquieting implications. If Bousset's view is correct, it follows that calling Jesus 'Lord' was not part of primitive Christian belief and practice. Here, one might argue, is Jesus, an ordinary man, who some fifteen to twenty years after his death began to be compared with pagan deities and called 'Lord'. The implication is that, if this is so, then the acceptance of Jesus as Lord was not a universal feature of early Christianity, and therefore it is dispensable; not only so, but the giving of a 'natural' explanation of how this belief arose may be sufficient to show that it is not necessarily a piece of divine revelation. The lordship of Jesus is no longer a matter of divinely-revealed truth.

Exactly this approach seems to be taken by some adherents of the current school of thought which attacks the idea of 'God incarnate' as a myth which should be done away with. It is argued that the doctrine of the incarnation is taught in only a few passages in the New Testament, principally late ones, that the development of the idea can be explained in terms of Samaritan mythology or by analogy with pagan myths and legends, and that traditional formulae about the person of Jesus do not enshrine truth revealed by God but are the result of Christian thinking in a particular historical setting (J. Hick (ed.), *The Myth of God Incarnate*, London, 1977).

Biblical criticism has so often reached conclusions such as

these that it is not surprising that it has been regarded as an enemy of Christian faith. We can identify four things that have happened:

First, the historicity of various crucial events has been denied. To make his theory about *Maran atha* work, Bousset had to argue that Acts 2:36, which says that Jesus was recognised as Lord by his followers as early as the day of Pentecost, is historically incorrect.

Secondly, the existence of diverse and even contrary ways of thinking about Jesus has been argued. Some Christians, it is said, saw Jesus as the Jewish Messiah, others as a pagan cult-deity. We have to choose one or the other, or perhaps neither.

Thirdly, the growth of belief in Jesus as Lord has been explained as a natural process under the influence of a pagan environment. The implication drawn by at least some scholars is that the doctrine of the lordship of Jesus is no longer a matter of divine revelation.

Fourthly, it follows as a result that the truthfulness of the Bible, and hence its status as the inspired Word of God, is impugned.

If we draw in many of the other conclusions of biblical criticism, we shall see that facts which to many people are part of the foundation of Christian belief are often denied or explained away. We are bound to ask whether there is something inherently wrong and anti-Christian in the whole task of biblical criticism. Surely the methods are wrong in themselves if they lead to such conclusions?

We shall attempt to find a way ahead by distinguishing three types of approach to biblical study.

1. There is the so-called 'dogmatic' approach which is sometimes thought to be typical of conservative students of the Bible. Here one simply records what the biblical writers themselves say about matters of authorship and the like, and for the rest ignores historical investigation. If Paul quotes Isaiah 65:1 f. with the phrase 'Isaiah says' (Rom. 10:20 f.), that settles the matter.

Sometimes this may seem to be a possible approach, as when people take at its face value the ascription of 1 Timothy to Paul and ignore any difficulties that this raises. In reality the approach is impossible. The statements from which such 'dogmatic' conclusions are drawn need to be understood historically. For example, we must ask whether it was possible in the first century for a disciple of Paul to write a letter in his master's name. Or again, if we ask where Paul was in prison when he wrote Philippians, we have to evaluate the complicated historical and linguistic evidence to decide whether he was in Rome, Ephesus, Caesarea, or somewhere else. Scholars who affirm that Moses wrote Deuteronomy but then separate off the last chapter because it inconveniently records the author's death are also practising a kind of literary criticism. In short, one cannot avoid historical and literary study. Although some people claim to be able to dispense with biblical criticism and to settle all issues by the plain simple evidence of what the Bible says, they still have to use biblical criticism to find out just what the Bible does say.

2. At the opposite extreme is the 'historical-critical' method. This is not the same thing as what I have broadly called 'historical study', but is a method based on certain specific principles. These were formulated by the German scholar E. Troeltsch, and in simplified form they are: (a) All historical statements are open to doubt. The historian must approach all the evidence in a sceptical frame of mind, and his results will only be probable and never certain. (b) We can and must work out what kind of things happened in the past by analogy with our own experience in the present time. All events are in principle similar. (c) Everything, but everything, that happens in history is governed by the laws of natural cause and effect. Miracles and acts of God are impossible.

Biblical study conducted on these principles cannot avoid regarding the Bible, a book about the acts of God, as untruthful and unreliable. From the outset the historical-critical method is committed to an explanation of Christianity which is different from that of the Bible itself. The assumption not simply that parts of the Bible may be false but that they actually are false is built into the method. To be sure, not all practitioners of the method are consistent. Some are prepared to accept certain supernatural events (such as the resurrection of Jesus), while others draw a distinction between what they may say as scholars and what they may privately believe as Christians.

It is sad that so much biblical criticism has been conducted on the principles of this method, since the association has led to the belief that it is inherently sceptical and unbelieving. However, what is wrong is clearly the set of presuppositions. It simply is not true that the historian must be sceptical towards all his sources. Taken to its logical conclusion this approach would be self-stultifying, since it would imply that the historian himself is unreliable – for surely he has no right whatever to consider himself more reliable than any of the sources whose reliability he questions. The historian must establish as carefully as possible what happened and test the reliability of his sources, but this does not mean that he must be sceptical of them all. Again, it is sheer assumption that nothing can have happened in the past which has no analogies in our experience. The central event in Christianity is the coming of the Son of God into this world. Because it is unique does not mean that it could not have happened. What right has any historian to declare that it could not have taken place? And, finally, it is pure presupposition that only 'natural' events can occur. To deny the possibility of miraculous events is nothing more than prejudice. In short, these presuppositions are all arbitrary assumptions, and there is no reason why we should feel compelled to accept them.

It is not surprising, then, that the historical-critical method has failed to give a satisfying explanation of the Bible. One must not condemn all its works out of hand, since undoubtedly much valuable work has been done by proponents of it, and we would be the poorer without what has been done.

3. We turn, therefore, to what has been called the 'gram-matico-historical' method. The name is a jaw-breaker, but is meant simply to indicate that biblical study involves both linguistic and historical study. The biblical text is to be understood in the light of its language and its historical context, and all possible methods that can shed light on the text are to be practised. It is this approach which is being commended in this book, for it is fully compatible with Christian belief and with the character of the Bible as the Word of God.

We have now reached the point where we can reconsider the questions raised by Bousset's study of *Maran atha*.

First, we saw that thinkers like Bousset wanted to portray the development of Christian doctrine as a natural process. But it is not necessarily the case that if we can produce a 'natural' explanation of a doctrine it is no longer to be understood as a divine revelation. If we can give a physiological explanation of a brain process, this does not call in question the truth of an argument produced by a brain process. 'Natural' and 'theological' explanations can be complementary and need not rule each other out. Suppose that Bousset was right in believing that the use of *Maran atha* was late and that Christians only slowly realised that Jesus is Lord. This does not mean that the development was not guided by God. In fact it is probable that there was development in the Christian understanding of the Lordship of Jesus, since Christian doctrine did not emerge fully-fledged on the day of Pentecost, and it is perfectly possible that the pagan environment of the Church provided some stimulus towards this development. The growth of Christian doctrine could have taken place in ways which are open to historical investigation and yet still be the result of divine causation.

However, it must be remembered that there is a distinction between explanations which are complementary, as in this case, and those which are contradictory. If, for example, it could be demonstrated historically that the bones of Jesus still lie in a grave in Palestine and that the stories of his appearances at the first Easter are one and all unhistorical legends, then this would certainly cast doubt on the theological truth that God raised him from the dead.

Such suggestions are sometimes made, and this leads to our second point. We need to keep our eyes open for explanations which are based on faulty presuppositions. If a scholar produces an argument which relies on the presupposition that miracles do not happen, then we can justifiably point out that the presupposition is questionable. It is not unknown for biblical scholars to measure the truth of the Bible according to what they consider that 'modern man' is able to believe and then to produce a watered-down version of Christianity that may be more palatable to him. While one must sympathise with the desire to remove unnecessary barriers to Christian belief, we must not let modern unbelieving man be the criterion of what Christians are allowed to believe.

Yet, when all this has been said, it is still the case that the conclusions of scholars may be independent of their presuppositions, and it simply will not do to dismiss unwelcome conclusions by attributing them to the bias of scholars. Our third point, therefore, is that we need to examine the evidence cited and the methods used by scholars to reach their conclusions. It may be that the evidence has been ignored or misinterpreted. This is the case with Bousset's theory that the Christian concept of Jesus as Lord was derived from paganism. What Bousset failed to do was to give an adequate explanation of the use of the term *Maran atha* with which our discussion began. Bousset believed that the Christian use of 'Lord' arose among Greek-speaking Christians in a pagan environment. He therefore had to explain away any evidence to the contrary, and in particular the fact that we have this Aramaic phrase in which Jesus is called Lord. So he devised his theory that this phrase arose in a bilingual church in Antioch and not among the earliest Christians in Jerusalem.

As far back as 1929, A. E. J. Rawlinson rightly laid his finger on this phrase and said that it was the Achilles' heel of Bousset's theory, the vulnerable point which rendered the whole theory questionable. Subsequent research has amply confirmed his criticism. Linguistic evidence has made the origin of the phrase among the earliest Aramaic-speaking Christians in Palestine – which was in any case always more probable than Bousset's far-fetched explanation – highly probable. We have already cited the case developed by M. Black and based on the Aramaic version of 1 Enoch. Whether or not one accepts his theory, other Aramaic texts from Qumran have conclusively demonstrated that the use of the term *Mar* to refer to Jesus was perfectly possible in Aramaic in Palestine.

The point that emerges is important. If one is dissatisfied with Bousset's theory (or any other theory), the way to deal with it is by the application of the grammatico-historical method, and not by dogmatic statements that he was wrong, or by simply rejecting his presuppositions. Although Rawlinson was in a position to criticise him fairly effectively fifty years ago, it needed fresh discoveries to establish the point more securely. The moral of the story is that the answer to bad biblical criticism is better biblical criticism, and also that the theories of yesterday and today can be upset for good or ill by the fresh-discovered evidence of tomorrow.

If Bousset's late dating for the entry of 'Lord' into the early Christians' vocabulary thus collapses, the consequences of his view also collapse. It is no longer the case that Peter's designation of Jesus as Lord in the early days of the Church must be rejected as unhistorical. (There are, it must be admitted, other reasons why many scholars doubt whether Acts 2:36 is a verbatim transcript of what Peter said on the very first day of the Church's existence, but space precludes discussion of these.) It is no longer the case that the theology of the earliest Christians in Jerusalem and that of the Christians in Antioch should be regarded as diverse or contradictory. We have no reason to believe that Christians in Jerusalem and Antioch disagreed with one another on this issue. Paul might reproach Peter on the question of Jews not eating with Gentiles – an issue on which Antioch undoubtedly came more speedily to an enlightened practice than Jerusalem (Gal. 2:11–14) – but there is absolutely nothing to suggest that they were anything but united in their understanding of the person of Jesus. It follows that there is no need to question the reliability of the biblical account on this particular matter.

I have deliberately chosen an example which demonstrates how application of the grammatico-historical method can help to maintain the reliability of the New Testament account of things over against other theories which call the truth of the account in question. Yet it must be firmly said that the use of this method will not remove or solve all the difficulties and problems that readers find in the text. One does not need to be a follower of the historical-critical method to discover apparent contradictions and errors in Scripture. The radical may look for them with more zeal than the conservative, but even the latter can hardly avoid noticing, for example, that there are two rather different genealogies of Jesus in the Gospels. There is nothing wrong with discovering such things, and scholarly objectivity indeed compels us to take account of them. The real question is how they are to be explained. In many cases grammatico-historical study may show that the alleged contradiction or error is not a real one, since a convincing explanation or harmonisation exists. In other cases such an explanation may not be immediately forthcoming. It is at this point that one may wish to suspend judgment, which is a perfectly legitimate thing to do if a theory seems generally sound despite the existence of some apparent evidence to the contrary. At the same time, however, it may be necessary to ask how the existence of particular types of problem may affect one's understanding of the nature of Scripture. The scholar who believes in the entire trustworthiness of Scripture will regard his belief as a well-founded presupposition which is relevant to his treatment of critical problems, but at the same time he will be aware that his doctrine of the nature of Scripture must be consistent with the actual character of Scripture.

The authors of the Chicago Statement were obviously well aware of this point when they proceeded to qualify their definition of inerrancy in the light of such undeniable facts as the free citations from the Old Testament in the New, and to insist that such apparent 'carelessness' must not be regarded as falling within the category of the kind of errors which would falsify their theory. Their understanding of inerrancy is shaped to take account of such phenomena. But consider another kind of example. Many scholars argue that the book attributed to Isaiah was written by more than one person, chapters 1–39 (in whole or part) being by Isaiah and the remainder of the book by later writers including an unknown genius known to scholars as 'Deutero-Isaiah' or 'Second Isaiah'. If, however, John refers to passages from Isaiah 6 and Isaiah 53 as both being spoken by 'Isaiah' (John 12:38–41; cf. Rom. 9:27 and 10:20 f.), does this mean that he specifically believed in the existence of one Isaiah, and are we compelled to follow his view on the matter? It is arguable that John was simply following the current manner of referring to the book of Isaiah and not making a specific statement about the identity of the author of its different chapters; if, then, critical study suggests multiple authorship, we are free to adopt such a conclusion. Others would say that John did believe in the unity of Isaiah, but he was wrong, and we are free to believe otherwise. Others again would say that John positively affirms the existence of only one author, and we are bound by his statement, no matter what critical study of Isaiah may say. Clearly what people like John and Paul believed about Isaiah is not irrelevant in coming to a conclusion about the authorship of the book, but if the weight of the evidence favours multiple authorship, then we are confined to the first two options mentioned. It perhaps does not make much difference which we adopt. If John was not making a specific statement about the authorship of the book, then we have to allow that there may be variety of opinion about the kind of statement he was making – whether or not it was a positive affirmation about authorship. If John made an erroneous statement in his ignorance, then this statement must be recognised to be compatible with the purpose of God in the inspiration of Scripture, and therefore is not the sort of 'error' which would conflict with the entire trustworthiness of the Bible; in other words, our understanding of Scripture must be modified accordingly in the light of the findings of biblical criticism. It may be, of course, that the problem of Isaiah is one to which scholars may give different answers. The point is that it is dangerous to adopt a view of the Bible which rules out the findings of honest, unbiased study.

To tread the path between the Scylla of suspending judgment on critical issues and the Charybdis of qualifying one's doctrine of the entire trustworthiness of Scripture is not easy. There is no simple formula which will enable us to solve all our difficulties. Faith is never free from risk or from the duties of self-examination and self-correction.

If, however, we are prepared to take this attitude, then we may with a good conscience defend ourselves against the objection that the methods of biblical criticism which I have discussed are cunningly contrived to avoid any possibility of our doctrine of Scripture being disrupted by contradictory or erroneous teaching. The objection is that, having subscribed to the presupposition that the Bible is entirely trustworthy, we then devise means to avoid any possible conflicts with this principle and to interpret any problem passages in a 'harmless' way. While some conservative scholars may be open to this criticism, it does not apply to all. It is entirely proper that, having formulated a theory of inspiration on the basis of the other evidence already discussed, we should endeavour to interpret the Bible on that basis and give it its proper place in our critical study; but at the same time if evidence shows up which militates against a theory or requires its modification, then we must be ready to alter our assumptions. What must not be done is to ignore or distort evidence that conflicts with our theories.

If after all this I continue to maintain my belief in the entire trustworthiness of Scripture over against some of my colleagues who find that the evidence conflicts with it, I can only say that this is how the total evidence appears to me. Nothing that I have discovered in close study of the New Testament over a quarter of a century has caused me to have any serious doubts about its entire trustworthiness for the purposes for which God has given it; I cannot claim that I have studied the Old Testament so closely. This is not to say that I do not have doubts and unsolved problems, or that I have not developed and modified my position over the years. I trust that my position remains flexible in the sense that it is not for any biblical student to be able to affirm in detail and once and for all just what is implied in God's inspiration of the Bible for his purposes.

Much of what has been said in this chapter has inevitably been concerned with the problems and dangers that conservative students find in biblical criticism. But the last word should not remain with this negative aspect of the matter. O. Cullmann has written some wise words about the practical value of the kind of study which we have been discussing (*The Early Church*, London, 1956). He points out that biblical study (he calls it 'higher criticism') enables us to take history seriously, to understand the human setting of the Bible, and to control our theological interpretations.

Some Christians almost dispense with history. Just as for R. Bultmann and his followers what matters is the message and not whatever historical events may lie behind it, so too some conservative Christians are content with the Bible as a divine revelation and are not very much concerned about the history which it contains, however loudly they may protest that they are concerned. Both groups are in danger of forgetting that God's revelation of himself came in historical events and persons as well as in the words of Scripture, and that what saves us is not the book which tells us about what God has done but rather the historical bearing of our sins by our Saviour and his historical resurrection from the dead. It is biblical criticism which continually reminds us of the historical setting of the Bible and thus of the great acts of God to which it bears witness.

Secondly, biblical criticism widens our understanding of the Bible as a human book, and hence as God's book. We may be in danger of ignoring the rich human variety which God has used in its composition, of seeing it simply as a source of doctrinal propositions instead of recognising the sheer human vitality of its contents and appreciating them as testimonies to the multi-faceted revelation of God.

Third, there is a danger that the Bible itself may be understood in a sort of vacuum, as a book written solely for us in our situation; we may run the risk of trying to understand what it is saying to us without paying proper attention to what it was saying to its original readers. The result is that we may interpret the Bible according to our own ideas and build up a theological system from it which is not truly derived from what the biblical writers were trying to say. Biblical criticism forces us to understand the Bible in its original situation and so helps us not to read our own ideas into it; by forcing us to attend to the historical, human elements in the Bible, biblical criticism opens our eyes to a fuller and better appreciation of the divine revelation which it contains.

This chapter has been written with those readers especially in mind who are suspicious of biblical study because of the dangers which they see in it. Certainly biblical study has often been pursued with results that are alarming to Christian believers and it has played its part in promoting unbelief instead of faith. I have tried to show, however, that we cannot avoid reading the Bible 'critically' if we are to understand it at all, and that such study need not be sceptical in its presuppositions but can be fruitful and helpful. This is not to say that I am advocating a biblical study which is biassed in the opposite direction and therefore lacking in objectivity. Conservative scholarship has not always been free from simply trying to justify its own presuppositions at the cost of objectivity. It is simply to insist that a self-critical biblical criticism is indispensable and that the devout seeker after God's truth has nothing to fear from it.

5

HOW ARE WE TO INTERPRET THE BIBLE?

Once we have established the original meaning of a biblical text in the light of linguistic and historical considerations, the task of interpretation is still incomplete. What remains to be done can be summed up by reverting to our discussion of the phrase *Maran atha*. What significance, if any, has this statement for today? Do we share the hope that the Lord will come? How does this hope affect our daily lives? Or, since nineteen hundred years have gone by and the Lord has evidently not come, do we have to abandon this hope or perhaps reinterpret it? The very fact that the phrase occurs in the Bible may well settle the basic answer to these questions for people who believe in the entire trustworthiness of the Bible, but it may not be so simple every time. For example, when we study the instructions for church order in the New Testament, we may discover that our particular denomination has not followed the implicit command in the New Testament to appoint certain leaders called 'bishops' (cf. Titus 1:5–9), or that we have gone beyond the New Testament in introducing leaders called 'churchwardens' who were quite unknown in the first century. Some people would in any case want to go to the opposite extreme and deny that we are bound to believe or practise all that the New Testament says simply because it is part of the Bible. One friend of mine said, 'I want to be free to say that Paul is wrong at certain points.'

We are concerned with the issues of 'exposition' and 'application' (as I shall call them), and they must be distinguished from the topic of 'exegesis' which we discussed in the previous chapter. Exegesis is the study of the Bible (or of any book) to determine exactly what the various authors were trying to say to their original audiences: just what was Paul trying to get across to the congregation at Philippi in his letter to them? Exposition is the study of the Bible to determine what it has to say to us. The difference between the two activities has been put in terms of finding out what the Bible *said* and what the Bible *says*. When we have discovered what the Bible *says*, there still remains the task of application, which is finding out how to put across the message effectively to any given audience. If I want to get across the fact of God's love for sinners, it may be appropriate to preach a sermon, write a booklet, compose a piece of music, or paint a picture. How I would speak about the theme would vary depending on whether I was talking to a dying man with only minutes to live, or to a sophisticated congregation of intellectuals, or to a youth group composed of youngsters with the haziest ideas about Christianity, or to a group of Muslims or Hindus. The message would be the same in each case, but the ways of getting it across would be very different.

We are not going to discuss 'application' any further here, but we cannot avoid a discussion of 'exposition' since this raises the whole question of how we respond to the message of the Bible as God's Word to us.

In the early Church there developed the belief that the Bible could have different 'levels' of meaning. The most obvious was the literal meaning or the surface meaning of the text. Sometimes the literal meaning seemed to be irrelevant to the reader or even unacceptable. This led to the suggestion that the text could have a deeper meaning, and three such levels were distinguished, the allegorical, the moral and the anagogical. Broadly speaking, the first of these expressed what we ought to believe, the second how we ought to behave, and the third what the future existence will be like. Not every passage was regarded as having all three additional meanings, and the lines of demarcation between them were rather vague; we may simplify matters by speaking of a general 'allegorical' or 'spiritual' meaning which could have different facets. A vast amount of biblical study in the Middle Ages was carried out on this basis. One can see the fruits of it not only in the writings of that period, but also in the stained glass presentations of the biblical story in medieval church windows and in sculpture, such as can still be seen most magnificently in the cathedral at Chartres.

The trouble with this kind of understanding of the Bible was that it was purely arbitrary and seems to have depended on the whim of the interpreter rather than on any principles which could be clearly drawn from the Bible or indeed from anywhere else. Often there was little connection between the literal sense of the text and the other senses that were read into it. No doubt the practitioners of this method thought otherwise, and believed that they were discerning meanings which God had deliberately hidden in the text for them to discover.

It is not surprising that the Reformation brought a reaction against this approach. The allegorical method had been used to support the teaching of the medieval Catholic Church. In their reaction against it Luther and Calvin insisted on the whole that we must go by the plain, obvious meaning of the text and not allegorise or spiritualise it. The Bible must be allowed to speak for itself and not become a vehicle for the ideas read into it by the allegorist.

What the Reformers had grasped was the principle that the exposition of the Bible is based upon exegesis. The significance of the Bible for us flows out of what the original authors meant to say to their original readers, and does not pass by it. The idea that God had hidden certain other ideas in the Bible which were not known to the original authors or their readers was firmly repudiated – with the important exception that a prophet might not fully understand the way in which his predictions of the future would be fulfilled. What the Bible has to say to us arises out of a fresh application to us of what the author intended to say to his original readers. (This is not to say that the original readers always fully understood what the author was trying to get over to them.)

This principle is absolutely fundamental to our understanding of the Bible. It has the effect of putting biblical study on an objective and scientific basis. In principle, commentators should be able to agree in determining what the biblical authors were saying. There will be disagreements over parts of the text which are obscure and ambiguous, but in general it should be possible to reach a fair degree of agreement on the meaning of the text. What the commentator is not allowed to do is to read his own ideas into the Bible. The temptation is admittedly always there, and modern scholars face it just like the allegorists in earlier centuries. For example, is it as a result of denominational bias that in the passage about the appointment of church leaders in Titus 1:7 some translations have the word 'bishop' and others 'overseer' or 'church leader'? And is it because of theological bias that some theologians interpret 'Christ Jesus who gave himself as a ransom for *all*' (1 Tim. 2:6) to mean 'Christ Jesus gave himself as a ransom for *all kinds of* people' and thus not necessarily for *all* people? Commentators must avoid reading the Bible under the domination of their own theological presuppositions.

Such presuppositions may be held quite unconsciously. They may reflect not just the personal idiosyncracies of individuals but the general outlook of the society to which they belong. The average modern reader of the Old Testament will probably concentrate his attention on the relationship between God and the individual which he finds there because his own cultural background predisposes him to do so. As a result he may overlook the importance attached to the community and to the actual land of Israel which is present there; the sacrifices offered at the Temple, for instance, were meant not simply to put the individual in a right relationship with God but also to maintain the holiness of the community as the people of God; or again, when a murder was committed, the land itself had to be cleansed from the resulting pollution by the execution of the murderer (Num. 35:33 f.).

If, however, the attempt can be made with fair success to determine objectively what the Bible said, what of its significance for the modern reader? Here the situation is somewhat different. The biblical writers wrote in a specific setting in the ancient world to specific audiences in their particular situations. But none of us lives in precisely the same situation as the first readers of the biblical books, even though we may detect many similarities between their situation and ours, and even though preachers delight to draw parallels between them and us, so that the biblical message can be applied to modern people. The result is that the biblical message may make no impact or the wrong impact upon us.

We all recognise that this is the case by the fact that we acknowledge the need for preaching and teaching the biblical message. If the Bible could address modern readers simply as it stands, there would be no need for sermons and Christian books. We would merely read the Bible or recite its words aloud, and that would be sufficient to make its message come home to us and our hearers. To some extent this does happen. There are plenty of examples of people being converted simply through reading the Bible without other helps of any kind. But in practice we recognise that this is not enough. And so we preach sermons, read commentaries, and hold Bible discussions in which we share our insights into what we think the Bible is saying to us. We implicitly recognise that something needs to be done to make the message 'come alive' today.

Strange though it may seem, sometimes problems arise from over-familiarity with the Bible. By a very young age most people with a Christian upbringing know the parable of the prodigal son so well that it loses all its force for them. They *know* right from the beginning that the father will welcome the wayward son back home and that the father typifies God. The father's forgiving love is taken for granted, and so the original force of the parable gets lost. But the first hearers, who had never heard the story before, probably expected that the son would suffer some kind of chastisement from his father – just as the son himself expected. They would listen with bated breath to see just what would happen when he came near his home again. They were in for a surprise when Jesus reached the climax of the story, a surprise that we may fail to experience, with the result that the story loses its intended emotional impact. It needs the experience of one modern prodigal to bring home the point to us. After his return home a friend said to him, 'I suppose your father killed the fatted calf for you?' 'No,' came the reply, 'but he nearly killed the prodigal son!' Perhaps that prodigal had expected to be better treated, but he was sadly disillusioned. Over-familiarity with the story can blunt our ears to its astounding account of a pardoning love which must have shocked many of its first hearers.

Nevertheless, probably most of our modern problems arise from unfamiliarity with the Bible and with the ways of thinking and the culture of the world in which it was written. We find it strange that certain foods could be regarded as religiously defiling, or that people were made religiously unclean by various physical diseases and bodily discharges, so that no Israelite was allowed to eat such food, and unclean people had to make a special offering to God to obtain cleansing. Yet we shall not understand much of the legislation in the Old Testament if we cannot appreciate this way of thinking; nor shall we be able to comprehend the catastrophic effect that it must have had on the Jews when Jesus and his followers began to abandon this way of thinking and the practices which went along with it.

It may not be all that difficult to deal with this kind of problem. People can be given the background knowledge of the biblical world which will enable them to appreciate the situation of its first readers and their ways of thinking and acting. The problem becomes more tricky when it is a case of sharing a way of thinking that is alien from our own and making it part of our own thinking and believing. In the Gospels we come up against people who are said to be demon-possessed. They behave in a way that we would associate with mental disorders, but in the absence of modern medical knowledge they are restored to a normal condition by exorcism, the driving out of the demon or demons whose dwelling they had become. Jesus and the early Christians shared this belief in the reality of demons and other evil spirits. Now we do not need to share the ancient belief in ritual uncleanness, since this has been declared null and void in the New Testament, but what about belief in the reality of demons? The New Testament certainly teaches that the demons may be conquered by the power of God, so that we do not need to fear them, but the reality of demons is not denied. Is belief in the existence of demons and the like part of the package which we accept when we become Christian believers? Some Christians would want to insist that belief in Jesus Christ as the Son of God does not necessarily involve belief in demons as well.

Other aspects of biblical teaching may seem to be contradicted by our normal understanding of things or even to be ethically objectionable. The Bible appears to accept the existence of a so-called three-decker universe – a flat earth with the underworld below and heaven up above – and this cannot stand in the face of modern scientific knowledge. To some people the idea of a God who needs to be reconciled to sinners by the death of his Son is morally unacceptable. Even the idea of a transcendent God is uncongenial to some people who would like simply to accept Jesus as a great moral teacher.

So what do we do if the Bible contains things that modern people find hard to believe? Faced by this problem people make different responses. Some are prepared to believe anything, simply because the Bible says it. Others insist that much of what it says is incredible and claim the right to pick and choose what they will believe. Still others argue that a message expressed in an unacceptable 'mythological' form can be demythologised into an acceptable one.

Many people who believe in the entire trustworthiness of the Bible fall into the first of these three groups. They may say that they have no problems, but, if they do, they deceive themselves. To begin with they may well be inconsistent in saying that they accept the biblical view of everything while they actually live in a different way. To quote the hackneyed example, when somebody falls ill, those who claim to follow the New Testament should probably attribute the cause to demon-possession and seek out a person with spiritual powers of healing rather than go to a doctor, yet in the majority of cases such people will undoubtedly go first to the doctor and also pray for the patient. Nor is it uncommon for such people to live in comparative luxury despite the fairly plain injunctions in the New Testament to sacrificial giving. Then, such people still need to find out exactly what the Bible is saying to them before they can adopt its teaching. There have been Bible-believers in the past who asserted on biblical grounds that the sun went round the earth and persecuted those like Galileo who taught differently; today it is universally accepted that the Bible does not teach that the earth is the centre of the universe. Or there are people today who insist on baptism by immersion on the basis of what is at least a disputable interpretation of certain verses in the New Testament. An attitude of readiness to accept and obey what the Bible says does not free us from the necessity of determining what exactly the Bible does say. We are back at the problem of interpretation.

As for the 'liberals' at the other end of the theological spectrum, here the problem is, as we have seen, the arbitrariness of their choice of what to believe or not to believe. It is, of course, open to an unbeliever to disbelieve whatever he wishes in the Bible and in Christianity (apart from those facts which can be regarded as reasonably certain in the light of appropriate forms of study). But the essence of Christian belief is that it accepts what unbelieving man is not prepared to accept about God, the universe and himself. To become a Christian is to turn from unbelief to belief, and thus to admit that one's beliefs are ultimately not controlled by the thinking and standards of the unbelieving world. So again the question arises: what exactly is contained in Christian belief? What is it that the Christian is called to believe? Again we come back to the problem of interpretation.

One solution, adopted by people who feel that these are real difficulties, is what has come to be called 'demythologisation'. According to R. Bultmann the essential message of the Bible has come to us expressed in the thought-forms of the ancient world. Ancient thinking was mythological, an adjective which Bultmann uses to describe everything from the three-decker universe to the resurrection of Jesus. He argues that scholars of an older generation (loosely known as 'liber-als') tried to pick and choose among the teachings of the Bible, rejecting those that were unscientific or otherwise uncongenial. Not only did they throw out the baby with the bathwater, by discarding the message of the Bible along with the way in which it was expressed, they also acted purely arbitrarily in what they chose to retain. In fact their aim was an impossible one, since for Bultmann the thinking of the Bible is through and through mythological, so that it is not possible to separate it into mythological and non-mythological parts.

Therefore, argued Bultmann, another procedure must be followed. If the thinking of the Bible is expressed throughout in mythological terms, then instead of jettisoning it all we should rather seek out the truths expressed in the myth and set them out in a non-mythological form. When Bultmann did this, he claimed that the essential message of the Bible could be set out in a different kind of language, that of the philo-sopher M. Heidegger with its distinction between inauthentic and authentic existence. Inauthentic existence corresponds roughly to the biblical idea of living in sin or under the power of the lower nature (what the Bible calls literally 'the flesh'), while authentic existence corresponds to the biblical idea of life in Christ or salvation. The way from the former kind of existence to the latter – and here we see the Christian faith of Bultmann coming to expression – is through Jesus Christ as he is preached in the gospel; it is the fact of Jesus that makes conversion to new life possible.

Here, then, is a total solution to the problem. Sadly, despite its good intentions, it has serious flaws. In effect it transforms the content of Christianity into a set of ideas about man instead of a message about the saving action of God in history. Bultmann is almost completely indifferent to histor-ical acts and especially to the historical facts about the life, death and resurrection of Jesus. They do not matter because it is the 'preaching' that brings salvation. The mere 'fact' of Jesus Christ should be sufficient for us without our knowing very much about him, and in any case Bultmann is highly sceptical of much of the contents of the Gospels. This means that there is really no way of telling whether the message is true or false, and no way of choosing between, say, Jesus and Buddha. Further, there is no room for actions of God, for these are mythological, and some critics have argued that Bultmann should logically have dispensed with the idea of God, although in fact he refused to do so; Bultmann's attempt to find modern language for sin and salvation is certainly helpful, but the rest of the Christian message tends to disappear from sight. For Bultmann the Bible becomes basically a book about man and what man must do, whereas surely it is more correct to say that the Bible is primarily a book about God and what he has done for man. Bultmann's translation of the Bible into demythologised terms loses far too much of the original in the process to be at all convincing.

Bultmann's approach is thus unacceptable: it misinterprets the central message of the Bible. Nevertheless, it may suggest to us an approach to interpretation which is free from this criticism.

1. First of all, we may take up the question of the commands in the Bible which are addressed to Christians. Among them are some instructions for slaves in relation to their masters (e.g. Col. 3:22–25). In their literal sense these instructions can no longer be carried out in the Western world since slavery no longer exists. What, then, do we do about these commands? We could disregard them as being no longer applicable. It is more sensible to ask what principles of conduct they embody and then to reapply these principles in our changed situation. In some cases we shall not need to burrow below the surface to find such principles. The command to do one's work sincerely in order to please God and not simply to do sufficient to please an employer (and skimp the bits that you hope he will not notice) is surely valid in any working situation. But the command to obey one's master in everything is difficult in a situation where it may be a condition of employment to belong to a trade union whose directives may conflict with those of the employer, and also where it is a recognised

practice that employees are to some extent partners in work with their employers rather than silent, mindless slaves. If we say that the biblical command means today that we should give appropriate respect and loyalty to employers rather than unconditional obedience, are we watering it down, or are we rather expressing the nub of the matter in terms appropriate to modern working conditions?

If this procedure is legitimate, what we have done is: (a) identified a biblical command which is not directly applicable in the situation of today, (b) sought out the underlying intention, which will probably be a principle clearly taught elsewhere in the Bible, and (c) asked how this principle is to be applied in practice in modern relationships. If it is objected that this method is somewhat subjective, it must be replied that this is inevitable, since there can be differences of opinion about how to apply biblical teaching to varying situations (just as there are differences of opinion about the mode of baptism).

2. Secondly, there is the question of biblical doctrine. Here let us look at two examples, both concerned with the forgiveness of sins. In Romans 8:34 and elsewhere Jesus Christ is said to intercede for us with the Father. This is a strange idea if it suggests that there is an unwillingness on the part of the Father to forgive us unless Christ pleads on our behalf. We know that it was the love of God the Father which gave his Son to die for us (John 3:16; Rom. 5:8). We ought, therefore, to see the purpose of this statement as being to assure us that if Jesus, the Son of God whose character was revealed to us in his earthly life and death, is on our side, then we can be equally sure that God the Father, whom we have not seen, must share the same attitude of forgiveness to us. In other words, the text is in effect saying the same as John 14:9: 'He who has seen me has seen the Father.' To be sure, this does not remove the need for faith that the God whom we worship has revealed himself in Jesus, but it does mean that we can cheerfully abandon the possible implication of Romans 8:34 that the Son has to plead with a Father who might be unwilling to pardon sinners.

Consider now a verse which says: 'without the shedding of blood there is no forgiveness of sins' (Heb. 9:22). This is a statement about the sacrifices described in the Old Testament, but the writer to the Hebrews applies it by analogy to the offering of the sacrifice of Jesus who shed his own blood. Many modern people find the idea of this kind of sacrifice (as opposed to the weaker modern idea of giving up something that one values dearly) to be quite repugnant. They cannot believe that God is unable to forgive sins without an offering being made, and they want to insist that God can forgive freely simply through his fatherly love for us. There is a strong desire to reject the 'without blood no forgiveness' principle from the Christian faith.

Such an attitude, however, would run clean contrary to a principle which is attested right through the Bible. In the New Testament it finds expression in the fact that sin is forgiven not by shedding the blood of animals which (as Heb. 10:4 goes on to say) cannot possibly take away sin, but only through the self-offering of the Son of God. Thus there is a cost to forgiveness, and that cost was borne by God himself in Jesus. The love of God can forgive sins only because it is suffering – and dying – love. Here we have a theological principle which, however offensive it may at first seem, represents an essential aspect of biblical teaching. To surrender this principle would be to surrender biblical religion itself.

The purpose in discussing and contrasting these two examples was to show that modern susceptibilities are not necessarily the key to what we may accept in biblical doctrine. We need to see whether there is good reason in the Bible itself for reinterpreting a particular statement or seeing it as the expression of a deeper principle. In the last analysis it must be the Bible itself which provides the criterion for interpretation and not our own idea of what is or is not acceptable. If a biblical statement seems unacceptable to us, the right course is to look at it in the light of biblical teaching generally, and this may shed light on it which removes the difficulty.

3. A closely related area is that of apparent contradictions in the Bible on doctrinal issues. A well-known example is the fact that Paul says that we are justified or put in the right with God by faith and not by works (Rom. 3:28) but James says quite expressly that 'a man is justified by works and not by faith alone' (Jas. 2:24). Here at first sight is a clear contradiction, and it can be argued that James is deliberately denying Paul's statement. Some scholars are content to record the contradiction and declare that it cannot be resolved. They then make a virtue out of necessity by saying that the Bible simply witnesses to diverse responses to God's revelation of himself and we are not bound by any of them. Those who believe in the trustworthiness of the Bible will ask whether the contradiction can be resolved. Superficially the two statements disagree, but at a deeper level they are in fundamental harmony. Paul's idea of faith includes the idea of its expression in loving actions (Gal. 5:6), whereas James has in mind a faith which is nothing more than mental assent to a truth. Paul writes the way he does because he is attacking people who thought that you could get right with God by trying to keep the Jewish law rather than by simply and exclusively trusting in God's saving action in Christ; James for his part was reacting to people who, possibly through misunderstanding Paul's teaching, thought that simply believing in God without any corresponding change in their way of life was enough to put them right with him. They are standing back to back, fighting against different misunderstandings of faith.

That is a fairly simple example of how one may have to look beneath the surface in order to deal with a contradiction in teaching. Some scholars distrust anything that smacks of harmonisation between contradictory passages, since it is easy to twist the meaning of one passage to make it harmonise with another. The warning must be heeded, but it does not mean that we should rule out the possibility of a fundamental harmony at a deep level in the biblical revelation.

Nevertheless, we should not close our eyes to the more tricky problems and their implications. In Deuteronomy 20:10–18 we have some directions for waging war: in the case of distant cities which resist capture, every male is to be put to death, and in the case of local cities, whose inhabitants might lead the Israelites into pagan practices, every living person and creature is to be slain. How can such teaching possibly be reconciled with the New Testament understanding of love and with modern, humane sentiment based upon it? There can be no doubt that Christians believe that the central teaching of Jesus and of his Church is that they should love their enemies rather than kill them and their families (Matt. 5:43 f.). There can also be no doubt that God must be regarded as consistent in his character. Must we not then say that in some parts of the Old Testament (and possibly of the New) we have a one-sided apprehension of his will by people who were not yet at the stage of fully realising his will and all its implications? With regard to the particular case before us it can be urged that the warlike practices of Israel's neighbours were considerably more cruel than those allowed in Deuteronomy and that the danger of Israel being infected with pagan religion and its low moral standards from the people whom they captured was serious. It may well be, therefore, that in this situation and at this stage of development the instructions given in Deuteronomy were as far as God could realistically take the Israelites, and that we should be glad that this passage shows some improvement on the war-customs of other nations and a clear expression of the need for avoidance of idolatry even at the cost of putting to death possible sources of idolatrous influence. The Christian reader may at least take to heart the warning against being affected by immoral influences – there is no saying how low modern people may sink in time of war – but he will love his enemies rather than slay them.

Here, then, we have an example of how some biblical teaching which contradicts a central biblical principle may have a particular function in its own time but cannot be taken on its own as God's word to people in another situation. Inerrantists may deny that later revelation ever corrects or contradicts earlier revelation, but they cannot very well deny that New Testament teaching does render some parts of the Old Testament obsolete as literal commands to Christians.

4. A fourth area of difficulty is where the biblical writers have a view of the world of nature which it is difficult for modern people to share, or make historical and scientific statements that appear to be erroneous. For example, the biblical writers probably did think of a three-decker universe with God dwelling up beyond the sky, a flat earth, and an underworld. There may be odd verses that suggest a more refined view, but it is most likely that the writers shared the common world-view of antiquity. But for us there can be no going back to that world-view, which may perhaps be regarded as an example of biblical phenomenological language (i.e. presenting natural phenomena as they appear to ordinary people rather than as they actually are). The problem, therefore, is whether any biblical teaching is inseparably tied to this world-view. Does the story of the ascension of Jesus demand that we believe in a heaven 'up there'? Surely not, we must reply. In a society which believed that heaven is 'up there', how else could Jesus be presented as returning to be with God? Here we have an acted parable of Jesus' transition to a new mode of existence in a way that his contemporaries could understand. In no way does the fact of the ascension depend upon acceptance of a three-decker universe.

The existence of Satan and demons raises bigger problems. For one thing, it is difficult to get a clear, systematic picture of the beliefs of the biblical writers and to distinguish them from popular superstitions which they may be merely reporting. It is hard to avoid the impression that there were varying beliefs at different times. If Paul had been asked, 'Just what is the difference between a principality and a power?' one feels that he would have had considerable difficulty in answering. The important thing is that in the modern world many thinkers have expressed their belief in the existence of an evil power or influence in the universe which is greater than the individual evil wills of mankind: call it the 'demonic' if you will. The biblical teaching is making the same point, that there is an evil force in the universe of cosmic dimensions. Maybe, therefore, we should see the biblical teaching as testifying to the existence of real, evil forces in the universe without necessarily being committed to sharing all of the popular language and conceptualisation which is used to express this belief. To say this is not to deny the possibility of such powers affecting individuals in the way described in the Gospels; modern Western man would be ill-advised to deny this possibility.

We have now looked briefly at four areas of interpretation. In each case we have been dealing with problems which arise from relating biblical statements to one another and to modern knowledge and practice. If we attempt to summarise what has been said, the first thing is that our modern situation with its beliefs and practices and with its critical study of the Bible is a relevant factor in understanding the Bible and determining its significance for us. However, it is not the ultimately decisive factor. The decisive factor is the teaching of the Bible itself, and we have argued that we must solve our problems in the light of an understanding of the Bible as a whole. It is the Word of God spoken in Scripture which is the decisive criterion for how we understand the various parts of Scripture. It is only by adoption of this objective principle that we avoid the danger of deciding what we shall accept as biblical teaching in the light of our own presuppositions and prejudices. When we say that a biblical statement or command must be reinterpreted in order to be significant for us or that it is now no longer valid in its original form, we may be guided towards this conclusion by our cultural setting, but the overriding consideration is the general thrust of biblical teaching which may or may not permit us to treat the passage in question in this way.

Secondly, our procedure has sometimes been described as seeking a canon within the canon, i.e. finding some central, authoritative strand of teaching in the Bible by which we may discriminate among its other strands. The most famous example of this is that of Martin Luther, who looked on the doctrine of justification by faith as the key to biblical interpretation and regarded the Epistle of James as 'a right strawy epistle' in comparison with the more 'evangelical' books because in his eyes it did not teach this cardinal doctrine. Luther's judgment was faulty and shows that the principle is not free from risk, but this does not automatically disqualify the principle. For in practice we all of us do work with a canon within the canon, drawing our main teaching from some books and passages and ignoring others. Most of us derive more basic Christian teaching from Romans 8 than from Romans 16 or Job 8. It may be difficult to define precisely what we mean by a canon within the canon, but the basic idea is a viable one. It must, however, not be misused. It is one thing to use the principle to disqualify certain parts of the Bible as Scripture and effectively to reject them as Scripture; that way is not open to us. It is another thing to use the principle to identify the central message of the Bible and to assess the place of the various areas of the Bible in relation to it, recognising that even the parts which appear to be right out on the fringe may still have some role to play in the total witness of the Bible. Here too it is worth remembering that some parts of the Bible which may seem to have very little to say to us in our situation may have a lot to say to other people in a different situation. When I suggested to a group of Third World students that Paul's teaching about food sacrificed to idols deals with a problem that we no longer face, I was made very much aware that it continues to be a real and pressing problem in some of their home countries.

Third, it has been implicit in what we have been saying that the Bible does have a message for today. However, it is possible that the ordinary reader may be tempted to despair of finding it after what has been said in this and the preceding chapter about the problems of studying and interpreting the Bible. He may well feel that the whole process is so complex to carry out and so uncertain in its conclusions that the Bible must inevitably become the preserve of scholars and there is no possibility of the ordinary Christian reading and understanding it for himself.

These feelings of gloom can be removed. It must certainly

111

be admitted that some aspects of biblical study and interpretation do need experts to carry them out. Translation is a case in point. Were it not for scholars skilled in Hebrew and Greek, we should not be able to read the Bible at all, and we thankfully acknowledge their efforts. It is also true that we are all helped by other Christians far more than we realise in understanding the Bible. Many of us are guided by Bible-reading schemes and notes which help us to understand our daily passage of Scripture. We profit from the expositions we hear from preachers and teachers, and they in their turn are helped by the books they have read and the courses of study they have undertaken. We ourselves help other people to understand the Bible, perhaps for example by some remarks we may make in a Bible study group or house fellowship. There is far more mutual help in Bible study going on than we may realise. For the Bible is the Church's book, and that means not only that it guides God's people, but also that God's people have a heritage of understanding handed down from the past and constantly increasing in the present time.

That is one side of the picture. The other side is provided by the well-known words of William Tyndale, the man to whom English-speaking people with no knowledge of Greek are more indebted than to perhaps anybody else in the history of biblical scholarship. He made the aim of his translation that the boy who drove the plough should be able to know the Scriptures. Similarly, the great scholar Erasmus expressed the desire that the farmer and the weaver would be able to cheer themselves with the songs of Scripture. These men knew that, once ordinary people could read the Bible, its essential message would be so clear and plain that they would understand it and receive the gospel. The Westminister Confession states the point more fully:

All things in scripture are not alike plain in themselves, nor alike clear unto all; yet those things which are necessary to be known, believed, and observed, for salvation, are so clearly propounded and opened in some place of scripture or other, that not only the learned, but the unlearned, in a due use of the ordinary means, may attain unto a sufficient understanding of them (1:7).

While there are problems in the Bible to keep the scholars busy, for the most part the essential, central message is sufficiently clear for all to understand. It is true that the message can be obscured and corrupted through misunderstanding, and the scholars are no more free from this than the ordinary Christian; that is why so much needs to be said about the right ways to study and interpret the Bible.

In the end, however, the Bible is a book that was written in the first instance for ordinary people. Despite the passage of the centuries and the undoubted difficulties that this brings, the Bible can still be understood by ordinary people. While biblical scholarship is necessary, it is not the case that only scholars can understand the Bible or that the scholars must come in between the Christian and his Bible. We all have to be prepared to apply our minds to understand the Bible, just as is the case with any book, but if we are ready to make the effort, then the Bible will become the means through which God speaks to us. The important question is really this one: what are we to do when we hear God's Word spoken to us through the Bible?

6

WHAT ARE WE TO DO WITH THE BIBLE?

Our discussion has moved through five phases, and it may be helpful to summarise the argument so far before we consider the practical conclusions to be drawn from it.

First of all we asked what the biblical writers themselves had to say about the nature of the writings which they already recognised as Scripture, and about their own writings. We discovered that some parts of the Bible were directly attributed to prophetic inspiration from God, in the sense that they contained statements which were believed to come directly from God; other parts of the Bible were composed as ordinary human works, but the writings of the Old Testament as a whole were regarded as divinely inspired. We saw that this understanding of the Old Testament was shared by Jesus. We also saw that there were indications that some of the New Testament writers regarded their works as having a similar kind of authority to that of the Old Testament.

Secondly, we took up the term 'inspiration' and looked for an explanation of it that would do justice to the character of the Bible. After looking at various views, none of which failed to provide some element of a comprehensive solution, we argued that inspiration is best understood in terms of the concursive activity of the Spirit through which the work of human writers could be at the same time a fully adequate revelation of God in written form. The actual means of inspiration cannot be explained; it included, but was not confined to, prophetic inspiration in the narrow sense. It stretched over the whole complex process of composition of the biblical books, and it embraced a very varied collection of authors and types of materials. Inspiration in this kind of sense is something that cannot be proved to be present, although various factors may point to its presence. Like acceptance of Christianity itself, acceptance of the Bible as the inspired Word of God is a matter of faith and not of proof. Nevertheless, such faith must be a reasonable faith in the sense that it must form a coherent part of Christian faith as a whole and must do justice to the evidence available to us.

So, thirdly, we asked how the fact of its inspiration would affect the character of the Bible – or, to put the complementary question, how we are to understand the nature of inspiration in the light of the actual character of the Bible. We argued that according to 2 Timothy 3:16 the Bible is said to be entirely trustworthy for the purpose for which God inspired it. But here we found differences of opinion among scholars. One school of thought argues that since God is the God of truth everything which God inspires must be true in every respect or 'inerrant'. We suggested that this conclusion is possible only if the result of inspiration is the same as if God had actually dictated the Scriptures word for word to their authors, but that this is to assign a meaning to inspiration which goes beyond the explicit testimony of Scripture. Again, we argued that the varied character of the contents of the Bible makes the application of the word 'true' rather complex. Further, we suggested that various aspects of the transmission and interpretation of the Bible, where God has chosen to leave us in some uncertainty and even in error may suggest that he was content with a lesser degree of precision in the text of the Bible than some modern scholars would like to find there. Finally, we noted that the Bible can be said to be 'inerrant' only if a number of items which might well be regarded as 'errors' by strict modern standards are so understood and defined that they would not count as errors by appropriate biblical standards. Evangelical scholars who are unhappy with the notion of inerrancy may be said to differ from their colleagues very much in the area of definition. They accept that the Bible is entirely trustworthy for the purposes for which God inspired it, and what a strict inerrantist might want to define as an error that would be incompatible with biblical inerrancy, would not necessarily be seen by this second group of scholars as incompatible with the entire trustworthiness of the Bible. In other words, advocates of this second position, which may be called a belief in the infallibility of the Bible, would insist that the inerrantists are perhaps claiming a greater degree of precision from the Bible than God has seen fit to give us. There is clearly room for differences of opinion, and the vital point is that both groups affirm the entire trustworthiness of the Bible as God's self-revelation over against any other view which argues that the Bible is untrustworthy in whole or in part. As with the inspiration of the Bible, so too with its trustworthiness and truth: it is a matter of faith and not of rational proof, since in the very nature of things it is impossible to prove the truth of the Bible.

Rejection of the truth of the Bible has often been associated with the practice of biblical criticism, and so this was our fourth topic. It is true that biblical study has often been carried out on the basis of presuppositions which deny the truth of biblical Christianity, and Christian scholars have sometimes been influenced by such presuppositions. However, we argued that it is possible to distinguish between the proper use of methods of linguistic and historical study and the adoption of sceptical presuppositions, and that believing Christians can use the methods of biblical criticism with a good conscience. Not only so: they must do so if they are to understand the texts fully in the light of their original contexts and composition. The right of the sceptic to examine the Bible as he would any other religious book (like the Koran) cannot be disputed; the answer to scepticism is not to ignore it but to do a better job. We recognised that biblical criticism may come up with conclusions that may seem to be at variance with our doctrine of the nature of Scripture. In such cases we must be prepared to examine our criticism in the light of our doctrine and our doctrine in the light of our criticism.

Finally, we moved on from discussing the original meaning of the Bible by grammatico-historical study to the question of its significance or meaning for today. Here we argued for the fundamental point that what the Bible *says* today arises out of

117

what it *said* to its first readers, and that other methods of establishing its present meaning (e.g. by allegory) are illegitimate. However, there are problems in moving from the past to the present, and we discussed how this transition is to be made. The danger is that the modern interpreter will be moved by subjective considerations in formulating biblical beliefs and practices for today, but we argued that this danger can be largely avoided if the interpreter understands the parts of the Bible in the light of its central message about Jesus Christ. Scripture must be interpreted by Scripture and not by our own predilection.

The time has now come to ask, 'What are we to do with the Bible?', and we propose to tackle it by an examination of the theme of 'authority'. To put the point briefly, once we have established the significance of the Bible for today, then the next logical step is surely that we should submit to what it says since it speaks to us with divine authority. But this answer needs some unpacking.

When we use the term 'authority' in ordinary speech, we generally use it in two ways. Sometimes we speak about the authority of a despotic ruler whose word is law simply because he has the power to enforce his commands. In a totalitarian state the decision as to what is a crime depends very much on the whim of the rulers who are able to apply various kinds of sanctions to ensure that what they want is done. Yet even in such situations it is hard for rulers to avoid using terms like 'right', and even harder for their subjects to refrain from thinking (even if they dare not publicly utter their thoughts) that the commands of their rulers are unjust and wrong. The subjects would prefer the exercise of an authority which is based not on force but on truth. However they may understand truth and right and so on, they recognise that there should be universally accepted standards under which even rulers stand. Such people have grasped the difference between authority based on force and authority based on truth.

Biblical authority is clearly of the latter kind. It is true that some people might argue that it is based on the dictates of a God with whom nobody can argue, since he has supreme

118

power. But biblical Christianity insists that God is the God of truth, and it is as the God of truth that he makes known his will to mankind. This is admittedly a simplification of a complex philosophical problem which cannot be discussed in the present context. It must suffice to say that the character of God as he has revealed himself is holy love, and that it is on this basis that we affirm as Christians that God's authority rests on his embodying this quality rather than simply on his possession of absolute sovereignty.

Inherent in what has just been said lies a second characteristic of the authority of the Bible. It is a derived authority and not an absolute authority. An absolute monarch has absolute authority; there is no court of higher appeal. But his officers who carry out his policies have merely a derived authority; they could not act if the monarch had not invested them with authority. The policeman has a derived authority represented and symbolised by his uniform. So, too, the authority of the Bible is a derived authority which has been conferred upon it by God in virtue of its inspiration. When a prophet spoke, his human words carried authority because he could claim 'thus says the Lord'.

There have been debates whether the authority of the Bible lies in what it says or in the fact of its inspiration. We accept some sayings as authoritative because their content is obviously true; we accept others more because of the identity of the speaker. It is common, though perhaps not altogether justified, for people to regard statements made by professors as somehow more authoritative than those made by junior lecturers, although in fact both groups may say exactly the same things. The difference, however, is surely that the professor may be presumed to have more knowledge and greater experience than the junior teacher, and therefore his sayings should on the whole have greater claims to be true. It is hard to see how one can avoid paying attention to the character of the speaker when dealing with statements whose truth may not be immediately obvious. Our belief that certain statements are true will inevitably depend on our belief that they come from reliable people. The authority of the text thus depends on the authority of the author, and in the case of the Bible its authority depends not only on the truth of its statements (where these can be tested) but also on the authority of its writers as men inspired by God.

We can draw a distinction between supreme and subordinate authorities. What a judge may decide in court is not necessarily the last word on a case; appeal can be made to a higher court and eventually in this country to the House of Lords. This does not destroy the value or the authority of the judges and of subordinate courts in their own spheres, always granted that appeal can be made to higher authority. It has been customary to regard the Scriptures as the supreme authority in matters of Christian faith and practice. To say this is not to deny the existence or the usefulness of other subordinate authorities within their proper spheres. The authority of the Scriptures, on the one hand, is concerned with Christian faith and practice. One may say, if one likes, that the Bible is the supreme authority on medieval European history or polymer chemistry, but the claim is totally empty, since the Bible offers no information on these and many other subjects. It may at best supply the framework in which other sources of information perform their functions. On the other hand, other authorities overlap with the Bible and may indeed have essential parts to play in certain areas of discussion. There are areas of human behaviour, such as euthanasia and the use of contraceptives, where Scripture has no direct guidance to offer, and the application of biblical principles must obviously be carried on in the light of information drawn from other sources.

Problems particularly arise in the case of other sources of specifically Christian authority. One tradition ascribes considerable importance to the private judgment of the individual or to the Holy Spirit guiding the individual. Another tradition ascribes high authority to the Spirit guiding the Church through its duly appointed leaders, such as the Pope in the Roman Catholic Church. Highly exaggerated claims have been made in the past in both areas, and the authority of Scripture has been placed on a lower level than that of the individual's Christian judgment or of the Church. In particular, it has been insisted that the Bible needs authoritative interpretation, and supplementation by the continuing tradition of the Church. Neither position is acceptable from the point of view of biblical Christianity. Each is correct in recognising that the individual and the Church have a part to play as subordinate authorities. But the point is that they function as *subordinate* authorities under the supreme authority of Scripture itself. Otherwise we are at the mercy of subjective opinions, no matter how much we may insist that the Holy Spirit still speaks through the individual and the Church.

But why do we need an authority in religion at all, it may be asked? We need an authority when we are unable to find out the truth for ourselves. When I go to the doctor to find out what is wrong with my health and to obtain a remedy, I am seeking knowledge in an area where I am to a greater or lesser extent ignorant, and I have to be prepared to trust the doctor as a competent person and put my well-being in his hands. My trust in him may be well grounded. I may see a certificate in his consulting room which guarantees his general medical competence (though it could have been forged), or I may hear the testimony of patients whom he has successfully cured (though that may be no guarantee that he can deal with my illness), or I may be recommended to him by other doctors (though they could all be in league to deceive the public). There are reasonable grounds for trusting him, although they could turn out to be fallacious, and I have to take the leap of faith. Human life is built on such structures of faith, and there is nothing surprising if our religious commitment is of the same kind. Where I cannot know things for certain by my own ability, I have to accept the voice of authority, and this is obviously the situation in matters of religion. In the end, therefore, my acceptance of the Bible as the Word of God, as the authoritative expression of divine revelation, is a matter of faith and trust.

But it is just here that many people have problems. There are areas where we think that we have the knowledge and ability to question what the Bible says. If historical statements in the Bible appear to be mistaken, do we not have the ability to question them? If we detect contradictions between different theological statements, have we not the right – and the duty – to choose between them? If we come across moral principles which conflict with our own principles (which may themselves be biblically based), are we not at liberty to question them? Here are areas where we may well feel that we have the right to exercise our judgment instead of accepting biblical authority blindly. May it not be the case that we are in danger of ascribing supreme authority to all that the Bible says instead of recognising that it contains a mixture of material of different grades of authority?

One thing is immediately clear. We cannot close our eyes to the existence of such problems and pretend that they are not there; we cannot suspend our mental and moral faculties. In many cases the statements made in the Bible can be assessed by ordinary human methods of study, and there is no reason why we should not look at them in this way. We may well come to the conclusion that the Bible is imprecise on certain matters, and we have then to ask how far this is compatible with our understanding of the trustworthiness of the Bible. As we have already seen, not even the strictest defender of inerrancy can deny that such imprecision is present.

In other cases, especially with religious and moral teaching, we still cannot avoid discussing the problems that arise, but in this area the subjective nature of our judgments is more obvious. We have to admit the fallibility of our judgments, and in particular we have to beware lest the values we uphold are drawn from secular sources and are ultimately non-Christian. In such cases we have to be prepared to subordinate our own judgment to that of Scripture. Thus we may well be tempted to set aside the biblical emphasis on the life-long character of marriage in favour of a view influenced by the less permanent and less formal relationships frequently practised today. It would be easy to claim that the biblical teaching on marriage was simply the expression of a time-bound culture. Yet, when we consider the biblical teaching about marriage in the context of the biblical revelation as a whole, there are good reasons for maintaining the biblical position however unfashionable it may be. And indeed there are various practical effects of modern customs – such as the increasing numbers of personal problems among adults and the frequency of delinquency among the children of broken marriages – which suggest that the biblical pattern is not arbitrary or time-bound but reflects a view of personal relationships which is inherently true and right. The biblical teaching is a healthy corrective to secular views, and it would be folly to abandon it.

This and other examples which could be cited suggest that there is a prejudice in favour of biblical teaching for the Christian. His problem becomes one of interpretation, that of recognising the fundamental principles given in a time-bound setting. He has to beware of rejecting as time-bound anything with which he happens not to agree. He lives in the faith that, properly interpreted, the Bible will guide him truly. Just as the patient has to trust the diagnosis of the doctor, so too the Christian must trust the teaching of the Bible where he cannot confirm it for himself; he recognises his own fallibility and is prepared to accept in faith the infallibility of biblical teaching. He may of course be mistaken in doing so – just as a patient may find that the doctor was not trustworthy after all – but he is prepared to take the risk.

All this is to assume that the function of the Bible is to give a divine revelation which we must believe and obey, or, more accurately, that this is part of the function of the Bible. But not all would agree on this point. Thus Morna D. Hooker has suggested that the Bible functions more like a set of signposts to help people to find their way; it contains in effect the record of a search after truth and describes the signposts which have been placed there to guide the seekers. But, she continues, often the signposts seem to have been put up for the benefit of people other than ourselves and do not guide us directly to the answers to our questions. What the Bible does, in this view, is not so much to answer our questions as to give us 'guidance in theological method' (The Bible and the Believer', *Epworth Review* 6:1, 1979, pp. 77–89).

To this suggestion one must say 'Fair enough'. It draws attention to an important aspect of the Bible. It does show us people trying to answer questions that are not necessarily identical with ours, and it does show how God guided them to the answers, and we can learn from the way in which they found their answers how we are to find ours. But this view falls short in not recognising that many of our questions are basically the same as those raised in the Bible and that the Bible gives not only signposts towards answers but also the answers themselves. It is a book of teaching as well as learning. It is true that we have to learn to use the biblical discussions of other people's problems in order to discover the biblically-based answers to our problems, but this does not weaken the authority of the Bible as a source of guidance for our enlightenment in our situation.

The danger in much evangelical interpretation of the Bible is that it can underestimate the 'humanity' of the Bible – its function as a record of human questions and searching after God. I am conscious that this criticism could be levelled against the balance of emphasis in this book. But the danger with the type of view espoused by Professor Hooker is that it diminishes the authority of the Bible, since she regards the Bible simply as an imperfect witness to the revelation and insists that the living Word cannot be tied down to the written word. However, a proper understanding of the Bible as the written Word of God does not tie revelation down in an unacceptable way. It is the Bible which is the Word of God and not our understanding of it. Granted that the Bible needs to be interpreted, it is still the Bible which remains authoritative and not our interpretation of it. For example, a book may be translated into another language and this declared to be the 'authorised' or 'authoritative' translation. But no translation can possibly be regarded as the final authority; it is always open to correction from the original, and the existence of a good translation does not mean that we can throw away the original as being no longer of any value. Perhaps the trouble is that some Christians have been prone to regard their interpretations of the Bible and their secondary statements, such as the Westminster Confession or the Thirty-Nine Articles, as almost infallible statements of what the Bible says. But the Bible remains the supreme authority over all such derivative statements. It was a Puritan (and thus almost by definition a conservative, evangelical Christian) who declared: 'The Lord hath yet more light and truth to break forth from his holy Word'. Acceptance of the supreme authority of the Bible does not tie down the Word of God to the Bible but rather leaves God free to speak to us in new ways from Scripture. The Word of God in the Bible is truly living and active, and sharper than any double-edged sword. It is an objective revelation, and yet it retains its freedom from being encapsulated in any human formulation. The accusation that conservative Christianity ties down the Word of God to the words of Scripture in an unacceptable manner is thoroughly mistaken.

So the Christian is faced by the authority of Scripture as the Word of God in its written form. He confesses its truth and its entire trustworthiness, even if he has to admit that there are uncertainties regarding its interpretation. In the Chicago Statement it is splendidly affirmed that Holy Scripture 'is to be believed, as God's instruction, in all that it affirms; obeyed, as God's command, in all that it requires; embraced, as God's pledge, in all that it promises'. If the Bible is precious to the Christian believer, it is not because it is regarded as a paper pope or some kind of magical oracle but because here one hears and receives the message of a gracious God who, having revealed himself supremely in his Son Jesus Christ, continues to reveal himself in and through the pages of Scripture. It is through the Bible that I know of the God who has declared his salvation in the life, death and resurrection of Jesus, and with deepest thankfulness I embrace that saving truth and stake my life on it.